MW00996608

Roadtrip with a Raindrop

90 Days Along the Mississippi River

Roadtrip with a Raindrop

90 Days Along the Mississippi River

Gayle Harper

Acclaim Press
MORLEY, MISSOURI

Acclaim Press
— Your Next Great Book —

P.O. Box 238
Morley, MO 63767
(573) 472-9800
www.acclaimpress.com

Book Design: M. Frene Melton
Cover Design: M. Frene Melton
Creative Consultant: Linda Palmisano

ISBN-13: 978-1-938905-63-6 — ISBN-10: 1-938905-63-6
Library of Congress Control Number: 2014907741
Library of Congress Subject Headings: 1. Mississippi River. 2. Mississippi River Valley. 3. Mississippi River -- Pictorial works. 4. Mississippi River Valley -- Pictorial works. 5. Mississippi River -- Description and travel. 6. Mississippi River Valley -- Description and travel.
Dewey Classification -- 977

First Printing 2014
Printed in the United States of America
10 9 8 7 6 5 4 3 2 1

This publication was produced using available information.
The publisher regrets it cannot assume responsibility for errors or omissions.

This book is dedicated to Love...in all of its flavors

*To Nanny and Poppy...*for recognizing my traveler's soul and setting it free.

*To Dad...*for teaching me to honor creativity and perseverance.

*To Mom...*for being the North Star of Love by which we all navigate, and the world's greatest cheerleader.

*To my daughter, Natalie...*whose strength, beauty, wisdom and spirit are sunshine.

*To my grandchildren, Alannah, Zachary and Mandy...*each a breathtakingly unique sunrise, reminding me that Love is endless.

*To all the rest of my family...*you enrich my life beyond expression.

*To my family of friends...*you are Love, manifesting in all of your quirky, steadfast, beautiful ways – I treasure every one of you.

*And to Mike, my husband, my best friend...*for holding my hand in the dark, for your sweetness and your steadiness, for your delight in rainbows and for being the pot of gold at the end of every one.

*Above all, within all, to that which enlivens everything...*the Source of all Love.

Contents

Foreword

As literature and myth illustrate time and time again, a river journey can be a life-altering experience.

Whether it's the young Buddha in *Siddhartha*, Mr. Kurtz in *Heart of Darkness*, or Huck in *The Adventures of Huckleberry Finn*, an epic river voyage teaches the traveler as much or more about himself than about the topography and geography of the waterway itself. It's an exterior trip that prompts an interior journey.

Fortunately for us, Gayle Harper's book, *Roadtrip with a Raindrop*, is both. While her encounters with the beauty of the Mississippi and the wide array of humanity who make their home along the river – barge captains, blues musicians, artists, hunters, historical reenactors and even a jolly nun – obviously move her in a profound way, she never fails to take us along to share her experience.

Like Vasudeva, the ferryman who helps Siddhartha find enlightenment in the rhythms of the mythic river, Harper acts as our ferryman, documenting the beauty of this mother of all North American rivers and its people in stunning photography and rich prose, while she herself undergoes the profound changes that occur when an artist meets her project of a lifetime.

The result is a beautiful, warm and intimate portrait, as stunning to look at as it is to read, that makes us appreciate all that the Mississippi River has meant and continues to mean to America. In these pages, we feel the river's pulse, we come to know and appreciate its people, and in doing so, we learn more about ourselves.

A river doesn't bestow enlightenment in and of itself – but it can provide clarity and insight for someone who was ready to observe and listen to it. Fortunately for us, Gayle Harper was prepared not only to learn and be moved herself, but she has the vision and the craft to make it as vivid an experience for us as it was for her.

– Bob Krist

Bob Krist has been a contributing photographer for *National Geographic Traveler* since that magazine's infancy in 1985. He also shoots for *National Geographic*, *Smithsonian* and *Islands* magazines. A three-time winner of "Travel Photographer of the Year," he's been honored at the Eisenstaedt Awards for Magazine Photography in New York City and has won awards in the Pictures of the Year, *Communication Arts* and World Press Photo competitions.

An accomplished writer as well, Bob Krist has produced beautiful coffee table books, how-to books such as the acclaimed *Spirit of Place: The Art of the Traveling Photographer,* and the New York Times bestseller *Tuscany*, in collaboration with Frances Mayes.

He generously shares his experience and wisdom by leading expeditions for National Geographic, by writing a travel photography column for *Outdoor Photographer* and by teaching at the Maine and Santa Fe Photo Workshops.

MINNESOTA
Cass Lake
Inger
Lake Itasca
Grand Rapids
Palisade
Little Falls
St. Cloud
St. Stephen
St. Paul
WISCONSIN
Minneapolis
Prescott
Hastings
La Crescent
La Crosse
Prairie du Chien
Guttenberg
Sinsinawa
Galena
IOWA
Savanna
Missouri River
Davenport
Muscatine
Burlington
ILLINOIS
Montrose
Keokuk
Quincy
Ohio River
Hannibal
Alton
St. Louis
Chester
Ste. Genevieve
Cairo
KENTUCKY
MISSOURI
Cape Girardeau
Charleston
New Madrid
Arkansas River
Holland
Tiptonville
ARKANSAS
Osceola
TENNESSEE
Memphis
Helena
Clarksdale
Leland
Lake Village
Greenville
MISSISSIPPI
LOUISIANA
Vidalia
Natchez
West Feliciana Parish
White Castle
Reserve
Darrow
New Orleans
Paulina
GULF OF MEXICO
Venice

America's Greatest River

The name "Mississippi" originated with the Ojibwe word *Misi-ziibi*, meaning "Great River."

The first European of record to see the Mississippi was Spanish explorer Hernando de Soto in May of 1541.

The Mississippi drains water from 41% of the continental U.S., making it the third largest watershed in the world.

Because the River is alive and constantly changing, it's nearly impossible to say exactly how long it is, but most measurements fall between 2,300 and 2,400 miles from the headwaters at Lake Itasca in northern Minnesota to the Gulf of Mexico.

At the headwaters, the River is less than three feet deep. By the time it reaches New Orleans, it's 200 feet deep.

The average flow of the River at the headwaters is six cubic feet per second. By Minneapolis, it's increased to 12,000 cubic feet per second. By New Orleans, the River is flowing at 600,000 cubic feet per second.

The River touches ten states as it travels from north to south – Minnesota, Wisconsin, Iowa, Illinois, Missouri, Kentucky, Tennessee, Arkansas, Mississippi and Louisiana.

At least 260 species of fish, 50 species of mammals, 145 species of amphibians and reptiles and 57 species of mussels depend upon the Mississippi River basin for habitat and nourishment.

Sixty percent of all North American birds – and 40 percent of all North American shorebirds and waterfowl – travel the "Mississippi Flyway" on their annual migrations, relying on it and on the surrounding wetlands for food and rest.

Eighteen million people, in 70 cities, count on the Mississippi River for their drinking water.

Native Americans have always depended upon the River's bounty. The Mississippians, an ancient culture of mound-building people, created cities with populations up to 20,000 people alongside the River. Today, many of these mound sites are protected and can be visited.

The River has always been a main artery of transportation. Today, about 487 million tons of cargo are shipped annually on the Mississippi. That accounts for 60% of all the grain exported from the U.S., plus millions of tons of iron, steel, coal and other products.

Barges are the most efficient way to transport heavy cargo. It would take 870 tractor trailers to transport the load that is carried by one towboat pushing its limit of 15 barges on the Upper River. On the Lower River, a single towboat often pushes 40 or more barges, each one filled with up to 1,500 tons.

Navigation is made possible on the Upper Mississippi, between Minneapolis and St. Louis, by a series of 29 locks and dams, which were constructed beginning in the 1930s. They are free of charge to all types of river craft and operate 24-hours per day.

Although there are countless differing opinions about the current health of the River and the best ways to protect and care for it, there is no doubt that it has been greatly altered and frequently abused.

The Mississippi River is one of America's greatest treasures. It is deeply embedded in our history, our present and our very identity. The better we know our River, the more likely we are to do what is best for her.

Prelude

Memory is a fickle and unreliable librarian. We are told that it's all filed away somewhere, but most it seems, cannot be found. There are rare moments, though, that seem to have been experienced with an uncommon awareness and so shine on, perfectly preserved, complete with sounds, smells and emotions. Such is the memory of my first sight of the Mississippi River when I was nine years old.

"Sit up kids," said Dad, "and look! We are going to cross the Mississippi River." As our blue-and-white DeSoto rattled onto a high iron bridge, my heart clutched and then soared and my mind simply stopped, overawed. I don't know where we crossed or where we were headed, but all the rest is as alive in me as it was in that moment. I can feel the rumble of our tires on the bridge and the vibration of it tickling me deep inside. I can smell the river's earthiness, see the vast expanse of murky water and feel its movement, its power and its mystery. It had me, completely.

When we reached the other side, it felt like I hadn't breathed. I exploded into a dozen questions, all trying to be asked at once. My parents answered what they could and then Dad said, "Listen, and I will teach you to spell its name." Then, in that voice he used when he had a joke to tell, when you could feel his own big, deep laugh being held back to meet your reaction, with his head bobbing from side to side, he chanted, "M…i…crooked letter…crooked letter…i…crooked letter…crooked letter…i…humpback…humpback…i." I repeated that until I'm sure my family would have liked to dump me in that river, but some deep connection had been recognized.

In all the years since then, although I have never lived beside the River, it has never left me. Hearing its name has always grabbed my attention as if my own name had been called out. Crossing it has always brought the thrill of seeing an old friend. I have always known that, somehow, my story was contained in the River's story.

The Mississippi is the aorta of our continent in every way. Since long before humans were here to notice, the great River has been nurturing the land and bringing new life. In the eternal cycle of water necessary for life on our planet, the Mississippi's essential role is to drain 41% of the land in the continental United States and deliver that to the Gulf of Mexico. Countless species of plant and animal life rely on its bounty. Humans, throughout our existence, have and will continue to depend on it for sustenance, for transportation and for the mysterious way it permeates life, brightening and enlivening it.

We all feel prodded by life at times to step off into the unknown. Sometimes we go willingly, sometimes we shrink back in fear and sometimes life simply boots us off that precipice, with or without our agreement. However it happens, once it does, I have never regretted it. In 1991, I left a perfectly good job to jump off into the unknown territory of freelance travel and editorial photography. Had I known more, I might have been afraid to try, but in my blissful ignorance, I jumped and I will be forever grateful.

In time, thankfully, there was a full calendar of assignments. I've had the good fortune to be sent to fascinating places around the world that I would likely never have visited. I've met people, from the secluded to the famous, who have shared themselves and enriched my life in ways I could never have imagined. Some assignments involved photography only, but some, and these quickly became my favorites, allowed me to marry words with the images and provide text as well.

In 2006, as my husband, Mike, and I were headed

home to Missouri after visiting his family in Wisconsin, we decided on a route that would keep company for a while with my old friend, the Mississippi River. When we came upon the Great River Road, a National Scenic Byway that follows the River from top to bottom, it brought the sort of awareness that tells you something big has just happened. I was smitten and I knew immediately I wanted to see it all!

Within days, there was a laminated map of the River on my office wall. I began watching my calendar for any opening and, when one appeared, I would stand in front of the map to see where I was drawn and then throw things in the car and go. Each time I fell more in love! I loved the River itself, its stories, its presence, its quiet power. I loved the people I met and the easy, lighthearted way they welcomed me into their communities and their lives. I loved what I came to call "river energy" – the way everything seemed just a bit more alive.

In 2009, I was surprised and honored to be nominated for the Santa Fe Prize for Photography. As a result, I was invited to attend the Review Santa Fe, a three-day whirlwind of one-on-one meetings with prominent editors, publishers and museum curators. The Mississippi River body of work, which had so far needed no purpose other than to inspire and exhilarate me, was now to be shared with others. The responses from reviewers and fellow photographers were exciting and there were several invitations for follow up, but in my heart I knew the project wasn't ready. I was waiting for something...some unifying concept that would give it bones and clarity. So, I gratefully declined and went back to work.

Six months later, while working on a photography and text feature about the Great River Road for *Country* magazine, I came upon a sentence on the National Park Service's website that changed my life. A single drop of water, it said, falling into the headwaters of the Mississippi in Minnesota, would travel the river for 90 days to reach the Gulf of Mexico. Every cell in my body felt the impact of that and came to full attention. It felt as if someone had hit the "Pause" button on the world. By the time I took my next breath, I knew what was happening. Although I had no idea how it could happen, I knew that I would make a 90-day road trip, following the entire Mississippi River, while keeping pace with an imaginary raindrop that I would call "Serendipity."

From that moment on, *Roadtrip with a Raindrop* has quite literally created itself and I have, happily, been along for the ride. It has been and continues to be an amazing adventure, constantly teaching me to simply take the next step and trust that all is unfolding perfectly. My job is to stay out of its way.

First, there was the issue of 90 nights' lodging – clearly beyond my budget! When I divided the river into 90 pieces, it averaged about 27 miles per day. Hoping that I might be able to stay two nights in each location, I looked for communities at roughly those points. Then, I drafted an email to Chambers of Commerce and Tourism Bureaus, giving a link to the work on my website and describing the project. "If you are interested in having me visit your community," I said, "and you can help with lodging, please let me know." I had no idea what to expect.

To my astonishment, responses poured in and, in the end, there were actually more invitations than there were available nights. With that generous support, the journey was made possible. As it turned out, it also added a dimension of rich surprises. Often, while making the arrangements, I was asked for my preferences and my answer was always the same. "Just a clean bed, please, and hopefully internet access," I said, "and beyond that, whatever you choose will be perfect." That led to an extraordinary itinerary of accommodations that helped me slide body and soul into the unique heritage and culture of a place.

There was a log cabin deep in the north woods and a fisherman's cabin on a pristine lake where I was alone with the loons and with Abby, the resident Golden Retriever. There was a tugboat converted to a B&B, a trendy downtown loft, historic inns, a sharecropper's cabin in a pecan grove and the master suite of a plantation mansion. There were also, in some places, wonderful people who invited me to stay in their homes. And once, unforgettably, I was handed the keys to a 30-room mansion and told that it was mine for the weekend – just enjoy and leave the keys in the dropbox when I go!

By August of 2010, it had all come together so effortlessly that I kissed my husband goodbye and headed north. Other than where I would sleep at night, there were no plans. I would begin at the headwaters at Lake Itasca in northern Minnesota and travel for 90 days, keeping pace with an imaginary raindrop on its roughly 2,400 mile journey to the Gulf of Mexico. I would take any road that beckons and simply let whatever happens, happen.

What did happen is that my heart was split wide open. As the river I was following grew from a fragile stream into a majestic force of nature, I passed through America's incredible diversity in geography, climate, cultures and lifestyles. And, in the midst of all the changes, I was shown every day that which does not change.

The River's powerful presence, while easily felt, is virtually impossible to fit into words. Dozens of people from north to south spoke of the River's draw, of its power to inspire them or to carry their troubles away. Its appearance changes dramatically, from tiny, wild and pristine to vast and muddy, but even when girdled, fouled and profoundly altered, its unchanging essence is instantly recognized.

So it is with the people I met. All the details of the way people speak, eat, play and earn their livings change continually, but everywhere I found the same openness, curiosity, playfulness and inclusiveness. From two-year-old Hazel in Minneapolis to 87-year-old Marshall Bouldin in Clarksdale, Mississippi, from city folks to "river rats" to cotton farmers and swamp-dwellers, I found beautiful people willing to pause in their own busy lives to really be with me. They told me their stories, introduced me to others, invited me to parties and barbeques, took me out on their boats or home to dinner and created opportunities that I could never have fathomed. The people of this journey are the soul of it.

Then there are the people who were part of the journey thanks to our marvelous technological era. I kept a blog as I traveled, called *Surrendering to Serendipity*. Although there was no time to promote it, friend shared it with friend and, by the end of the journey, there had been nearly 20,000 views from people all over the world. I felt them beside me, curious, inspired, marveling at what we discovered. Since I came home, thousands more have joined the adventure by following the blog, supporting the Kickstarter campaign, and interacting on Facebook and other social media. The outward ripples from one little raindrop.

Now, you hold *Roadtrip with a Raindrop* in your hands. In the pages that follow, words and images arise together to take you on the road trip of a lifetime. You can leave your agenda and your stress behind and set your spirit free. You can give yourself over to the wise guidance of our little raindrop, Serendipity, as she leads us through America's heart. You may learn things about our greatest river that help you to see it in new ways. You may feel your own connection with it deepen as you see how inextricably intertwined it is with our history and our very identity. You might, also, feel an expanded appreciation for the incredible diversity of our land and her people.

And...you might, as I did, find your heart bursting wide open in unexpected ways. Welcome to the journey of a raindrop!

Love,

Gayle

Chapter One: The First Ten Days

“ We are a country rich with natural wonders, but none is as central to our history or our identity as the Mississippi River. ”

– Gayle Harper

The Omen

First light pencils in the shapes of boulders strewn across the little stream. Dimension and detail fill in as the sunrise is painted in pale gold and peach. Worn smooth by decades of moving water and by millions of hands and feet, the glistening boulders lie where the men of the Civilian Conservation Corps placed them in the 1930s.

Later, there will again be families snapping pictures of one another clambering over the rocks. Someone will be helping a child make a memory or an old person fulfill a dream by crossing the Mississippi River on foot. For now, I am alone, witnessing the birth of a legend.

The baby Mississippi River springs from the side of Lake Itasca, deep in the pristine north woods of

“ A single drop of water falling into the headwaters of the Mississippi in Minnesota will travel the River for 90 days to reach the Gulf of Mexico. ”

Minnesota, about 20 miles north of Park Rapids. Around 500,000 people come each year to see the source of America’s greatest river and to earn the right to say, “I walked across the Mississippi River.” They will read the famous sign to their children and gather around it for photos. “Here,” it says, “1,475 feet above the ocean, the mighty Mississippi begins to flow on its winding way 2,552 miles to the Gulf of Mexico.” They may catch a bit of water in a jar to take home. Likely, they will remind each other of some downriver spot they know, marveling that this gentle creek will grow into such an immense force of nature. We are a country rich with natural wonders, but none is as central to our history or our identity as the Mississippi River.

For me, this moment is the apex of months of planning. Nearly a year ago, I read the sentence on the National Park Service website that stopped my world and sent it spinning in a new direction. A single raindrop, it said, falling into the headwaters of the Mississippi will travel the River for 90 days to reach the Gulf of Mexico. I knew then, without question, that this moment would come – that I would be here, watching the sun rise on the first day of my own 90-day journey keeping pace with a raindrop on its way to the Gulf.

Itasca State Park, Minnesota’s oldest and one of its largest, cradles and protects not only the headwaters of the Mississippi, but also precious remnants of the old growth forest that once blanketed the state. While the morning is still soft and moist, I decide to drive the 11-mile Wilderness Loop, a one-lane road through this ancient forest.

I am alone on the road, which is a tunnel at times through a towering canopy of trees. There are rare, virgin stands of red and white pine, maple, birch and oak trees, some over 100 feet tall and 300 years old. They fill the crisp, piney air with an unmistakable presence, which is both background and audience for a symphony of birdsong. I put down all the windows and ease along slowly.

Ahead, there is something big and black in the road. I slow the car to a creep and roll toward it. Because a man that I met yesterday described this creature in vivid detail, I know immediately what I am seeing. It is a magnificent black Timber Wolf. He does not move. He stands erect, watching me, fearlessly. I freeze, locked in his gaze, holding my breath. I feel him. I feel his wildness, his lithe, fierce grace and his dominion in this wooded kingdom. Time feels suspended and there are no thoughts.

Then, without the slightest preparatory movement or effort, he seems to fly off the pavement and vanishes. I stare into the forest and see nothing – no underbrush wobbles from his passing. He is gone.

I gasp for breath and tearfully whisper, "Thank you. Thank you."

Later, I meet my new friend who told me of the Timber Wolf. Because of its unusual solid black color and because a Timber Wolf's territory can easily encompass a 10-mile radius, he is certain that it is the same animal he saw several weeks ago. Many people, he tells me, live out their lives here without ever seeing one of these smart and wary animals.

"I believe," he says in a low, quiet voice, "that this is a very good omen for your journey."

I know the truth of that.

Terry

In the Ozarks, where I live, some folks would call this downpour "a real toad-strangler." The wipers are knocking themselves out, but I can barely see. Still, I was given good directions, so I find without trouble the little country store and make a dash for its coziness. It smells of fresh coffee and something like a mix of leather and cinnamon. When I tell the clerk I am here to meet a man named Terry Larson, she grins broadly and says, "Oh sure – we know Terry well. He'll be along soon." Last night, when I mentioned his name at the resort where I am staying, it brought a similar response – he's a bit of a legend, it seems.

Someone at the Chamber of Commerce told Terry about the raindrop journey and, although he said he doesn't usually do such things, something about it moved him to call and offer to show me around. Terry operates Northern Adventures Guide Services, taking people hiking, canoeing, camping, fishing and hunting in this unspoiled wilderness that is his home. His family's land, inherited from their grandparents, is some of the first to be touched by the baby Mississippi River after it leaves the protection of Itasca State Park.

I like him the instant I see him come in the door – he has gentle, playful eyes and a boyish smile that ignites his entire face. "We'll see what we can and hope that the rain lets up," he says, so we run for his truck with coffee in hand. He shows me the little one-room schoolhouse where he and his siblings earned the nickname of "the lard-bucket Larsons" because of the recycled lard buckets that they all carried as lunch pails. He takes me to the first public canoe access on the young and fragile Mississippi. It was created in honor of his grandparents and, with obvious pride, he points out the sign inscribed with their names. We sit quietly for a few moments, watching the rain splatter on the River, which is still less than a dozen feet wide.

We bounce along muddy, rutted forest roads as he points out wildflowers and plants and tells me their names, their medicinal uses, their life cycles, how they interact with their neighbors and which animals enjoy eating them. He brakes hard when he spots an osprey on a stump and we watch in hushed wonder as it rips great chunks of flesh from the prey beneath its talons. As the rain abates, he stops to check on patches of wild

“The Ojibwe ancestors who migrated from the east in the 14th century stopped here because the Creator had told them to travel ‘until they came to a place where food grows upon the water.’ ”

plums, wild grapes and high bush cranberries that he is watching, waiting for the perfect color to tell him that they are ready to be picked. Once, he stops so abruptly that it startles me, and he leaps from the truck, grabbing a white cloth as he goes. When he returns, he gently unwraps his prize and says, “These are perfect – absolutely perfect Western Puffball Mushrooms. I will make you dinner tonight.”

I’ve known plenty of “outdoor people,” but I’ve never known anyone quite like Terry. He moves through the natural world like a bear or a heron, diving into a thicket or wading into marsh without the slightest hesitation. When I ask about ticks or poison ivy, he smiles gently and says, “They just don’t bother me.” When he hears a grouse drumming or sees the first hint of red tingeing the maple leaves, his delight is unrestrained and contagious. He is constantly teaching, presenting each discovery as if it is as new to him as it is to me.

Late in the day, we pass through a locked gate and jounce our way up a long hill to the small, vintage trailer that he keeps on their property and he prepares an amazing meal of nature’s gifts. As he cooks, I enjoy a glass of wild berry wine and listen to some hauntingly lovely music from a CD called *American Rivers*, which was produced by the National Park Service and includes background sounds of water, insects and birds, recorded by Terry from his canoe. Dinner is northern pike, caught and smoked by Terry, served with a dab of tangy jelly made from the wild high bush cranberries. There is nutty, aromatic wild rice harvested from the Mississippi River and there are the absolutely divine sautéed wild mushrooms. Every bite incredible! Then, as if all this were not more than enough, Terry tells me that tomorrow we will canoe this wild and pristine River, and in the evening I am invited to meet his wife, Mary, at their home in Cass Lake for a fish fry. I hardly know what to say in response to such kindness.

In places, the River is just a narrow pathway through tall marsh grasses. As Terry paddles us through, I am keenly aware of how few people have the opportunity to visit this intimate part of the River. We gather berries as we go and, when we glide into a stand of feathery-topped wild rice plants, he brings out his ricing poles to show me how it is harvested. When the grains are ripe in a few weeks, he will gather it as the native people of the Ojibwe tribe have done for centuries, by bending the plants with one pole and sweeping the grains into the boat with the other. It is the sacred and staple food of the tribe, he explains, and is the very reason that they live in this region. The Ojibwe ancestors who migrated from the east in the 14th century stopped here because the Creator had told them to travel “until they came to a place where food grows upon the water.”

The primal beauty around us is at once elaborate and supremely simple. It hushes me with a sense of reverence, and I sense that Terry feels the same. We are silent for long stretches and the only sounds are the birds, the insects and the rhythmic dip of the paddle into the water.

When I meet Mary in the evening, she is exactly the gentle, genuine, content and gracious woman that I knew she would be. We all know that a lasting friendship has been created and we make plans for them to visit Mike and me in Missouri in the spring.

There are no goodbyes as I leave, only an echoing of Terry's trademark words, "See you downriver, my friend."

Cass Lake Morning

The alarm yanks me from a dream; I reach for it, but it slips away, leaving only a sense of movement that feels like dancing or flying. I lie still and listen – rain is strumming the roof of my cabin, so, in sweet surrender, I burrow back under the quilt. An hour later I wake again to birdsong and soft, silvery light, and I open the front door to let it in. I make tea, scoot the voluminous overstuffed chair in front of the picture window and curl up to watch the mist rise from the lake.

"The Mississippi River is out there, although it can't be seen. It enters Cass Lake on the west, flows invisibly through its heart and reappears on the east."

The Mississippi River is out there, although it can't be seen. It enters Cass Lake on the west, flows invisibly through its heart and reappears on the east. Stony Point Resort is full to capacity on this last weekend before the start of school and my little cabin is as comfortable as the ancient denim shirt I'm wearing.

Proud fishermen with their bounty smile up from the pages of the scrapbook on the table, some standing in front of this cabin as it looked in 1942. The walls seem permeated with the memories of decades of laughing, teasing, card-playing, fish-frying, sand-tracking families. The wooden screen door sticks open and, each time I come through it, I hear the echoes of hundreds of moms admonishing kids to leave the mosquitoes outside.

Last night, I stood on the swimming dock after the pack of shrieking kids deserted it and before the squadrons of mosquitoes arrived, watching the sun sink behind the lake. Now, the dock is a fluttery white carpet of seagulls, jostling one another for position. I let the big, soft chair envelope me and close my eyes for a morning meditation.

When I open them again, a little barefoot boy is outside in his pajamas, studiously pushing his toy lawn mower and paying particular attention to the puddles. A big brother is pushing his sister on the swing. A pair of squirrels is harassing each other mercilessly and the gulls still rule the swimming dock. It seems a second cup of tea is in order.

Somewhere, a man is singing in a groggy baritone, something off-tune that sounds like a polka. I can't hear the lyrics, but I am sure they are raucous – a woman is laughing. The breeze is bacon-scented. At the dock, a threesome of little kids, making what sounds like chicken noises, wave their arms at the seagulls. The gulls shuffle around and then, conceding it is time to move on, lift off in a great upward spiral, flashing white in the morning light. The kids march away, puffing their chests and swinging their arms in triumph. The man who was singing is now mooing, barking and crowing – no doubt entertaining a grandchild. A dad and his boy pass by with matching hats and fishing poles on their shoulders.

I have been an appreciative audience to it all. Now, the day feels like a skinny-legged girl, dancing with excitement and holding a surprise behind her back. It's time to see what she has in store!

The Powwow

It seems impossible that this morning I wore three jackets against the chill. Now, the sun is a huge yellow orb, bearing down from a cloudless sky with a no-nonsense intensity. With September a few days away, August is asserting itself mightily.

I'm on an unshaded wooden bleacher on the Leech Lake Reservation near the Ojibwe community of Inger, Minnesota. In front of me, the Cha Cha Bah Ning Powwow is underway. Dancers in brilliant regalia circle the drummers in an endless river of color, feathers, fur, shells and flowing fringe. The dancers, erect and dignified, are of both genders and all ages. Their expressions are stoic or peaceful or softly focused somewhere else. Their moccasins touch the ground gently, even the largest among them step lightly, some dipping and swirling and others moving only their feet. The bells on their ankles and dresses create a layer of sound like water on rocks, flowing beneath the drums. The cadence draws everything, including my own heartbeat, into its rhythm.

"Dancers, remember we have water for you under the tent. It's a hot afternoon," the announcer warns for the fourth time in an hour. "Please stay hydrated." I watch the sweat glistening on the muscular arms of a young man whose head is nearly engulfed by a massive bear headdress and a very old man who has danced continuously for an hour. They are oblivious, it seems, or accepting of the blistering heat.

The drumming stops; the announcer thanks the drummers and dancers and calls for a 30-minute break. I feel a bit disoriented and decide I need water as well. As I stand up, a woman approaches and calls me by my name. I'm startled, but she tells me that this is a good time to meet the man of their tribe that she had mentioned on the phone. Yesterday, I had called to confirm that the event was open to the public and I was assured that it is. I wonder briefly how she knew me, but then realize that I have seen no other obvious "visitors." She leads me around the outside of the circle, then points to a man and says, "There," and walks away. I wait until he finishes his conversation, then approach and introduce myself. I explain what I am doing and that it has been suggested that I speak with him. He nods and motions for me to follow him. We take chairs in the back of a booth where young people are selling soft drinks from a row of coolers. Then he looks at me impassively and waits.

I tell him about the journey of a raindrop and give him a postcard. I would like to understand more about the Ojibwe culture and history, I explain, because of its essential place in the story of this region. He lowers his chin a notch and looks at me a long moment with an expression that I cannot read. Then he speaks for the first time. "In our tradition," he says sternly, "when you ask someone for something, such as information, you first offer a gift of tobacco or rice." I am so surprised that the only response I can at first manage is, "Oh," while I quickly do a mental inventory. I have nothing but camera gear and a fairly squished energy bar. "I'm sorry," I say, embarrassed. "I didn't know and I have nothing to give." His expression has not changed. "That's fine," he says and pauses. Then, "It's hard to explain Indian to an outsider." At that, I sit very still, suddenly feeling my "outsiderness" and simply waiting to see what will be said next, by whom.

After a long moment, he begins to speak. There is stiffness in his manner as he says, "Our people are still here, after 400 years of oppression by Europeans. We still have our ways of governing ourselves and our spiritual and cultural traditions, and we are proud of that." When he speaks about the powwow, how it connects people and strengthens families, his manner softens a bit. I can feel him reading me.

Then he tells me of his work with the public school system, teaching the Ojibwe language and helping students with special needs. Mostly, he says, it's making connections with kids so that if they need help, they know that someone is there for them. As he begins to speak about his own seven children, he visibly relaxes in his chair and, when he describes their fine character and their accomplishments, a slight smile appears around his dark eyes.

Gradually, the chilly formality that was present when we sat down has dissipated and, as he says, "What pleases me most is that my children are each finding what makes them happy," he sounds like any proud father. He points out some of his children who are selling drinks nearby and some who are relaxing in the shade with friends. There is a sense of ease now and the perceived barrier between insider and outsider is no longer between us – instead we are just two humans sitting and talking.

The drumming resumes and he leans forward slightly and says quietly, "That is the heartbeat of Mother Earth. The water is her blood. The Creator looks down and sees that we are still drumming and dancing and singing the old songs and is pleased."

"That is the heartbeat of Mother Earth. The water is her blood. The Creater looks down and sees that we are still drumming and dancing and singing the old songs and is pleased."

"It's good," he says softly. "It's a good time to be Native. We have our rights again. We have the River to fish and swim and gather rice and we have the land to hunt. We have our drums and our songs and our community. We teach our children to be loving adults. What else is there?"

What else indeed.

I, however, will go shopping tomorrow and not be caught without tobacco or rice again.

Ghosts

At the entrance to the Forest History Center near Grand Rapids, Minnesota, I hear music coming from the woods. It's a tune from another time, lively, yet somehow mournful. I follow the sound, taking a path canopied by tall pine trees and find a lanky, gray-bearded man sitting on a log, playing his "squeezebox." When he finishes, he explains that such music was the only entertainment available for the men who lived in logging camps like the one recreated here. "They would dance with each other," he says, "because there weren't many womenfolk around." I take a seat on his log and he begins to describe life as it was for lumberjacks in the north woods in 1900.

When the first settlers of European descent came to what is now Minnesota in the 1820s, they found forests of centuries-old pine and hardwood trees so vast that they must have seemed endless and indestructible. Change, however, came more quickly than anyone could have imagined. Lumbermen, who knew the value of the trees and who had acquired the skills to harvest them in New England's forests, were moving down the St. Croix River, harvesting trees along the banks as they came. White pines, which were plentiful in this region, were the favored trees because their wood was durable, lightweight and floated well – and the Mississippi River would be the thoroughfare.

The region's first sawmill was built in 1839 and another quickly followed in 1840. As word spread that immense fortunes could be made, the forests began to fill with thousands of men, their horses and their equipment. America, which was growing rapidly at the time, had an insatiable appetite for lumber and the industry was fueled by an unprecedented construction boom. By 1900, the year frozen in time at this recreated logging camp, more than 20,000 lumberjacks and 10,000

"In less than 70 years, 3.5 million acres of primeval, old-growth forest had been decimated."

draft horses lived in the north woods in camps like this one. They were hastily constructed compounds of buildings, used for a year or two until the surrounding forest was depleted, then abandoned when the whole unit moved on.

During the long, brutal winters, trees were felled and the trunks were loaded onto horse-drawn sleighs and hauled to the banks of the frozen Mississippi River. In the spring, when the ice began to crack and move, men called "river pigs" set off, riding the logs downriver to mills like those in the growing town of Minneapolis. They worked from dawn to dusk, balancing on the rolling and lurching logs in the frigid current, using long poles to push away from obstacles. Their meals were prepared on a floating barge called a "wanigan," and were brought to them on the river bank, where they slept, exhausted, in their cold, wet clothes and then got up to do it again. It was grueling, miserable and extremely dangerous work.

In one year, 1900, more than 2.3 billion board feet of lumber were cut from Minnesota's woods and everyone knew that the forests were vanishing at an astounding pace. Although a few voices called for more careful methods, the profit-fueled momentum was a runaway train. Throughout the next decade, as lumber became harder to find and the quality declined, production fell drastically and, by 1910, it was all over. In less than 70 years, 3 ½ million acres of primeval, old-growth forest had been decimated.

The mindless clear-cutting left the land littered with tree tops and branches, known as "slash," and took only the marketable trunks. As the slash dried, the land became a vast tinder pile, vulnerable to any spark from lightning or a passing train. Great, uncontrollable fires raged over areas as large as 350,000 acres, destroying dozens of communities and killing hundreds of people. Farmers, who had often been told that "the plow follows the ax," tried cultivating and planting the cleared land, but most crops failed because of poor soil and short growing seasons. The beauty and resources of Minnesota's great forests had been devoured by greed.

The logging camp is quiet now and there seems to be no one around as I walk through the horse barn, the blacksmith shop and the cook house. The bunk house, which was called the "sleep camp," is dark and chilly even in August. I think about the men who would have slept here, their bunks layered in rows, dreaming of home. I imagine their weariness, loneliness and determination and I think of their families at home, wondering if their loved one will return to them.

I'm taking some shots when, through the viewfinder, I see the ghostly shape of a lumberjack in the doorway, partially dissolved by the brightness behind him. I'm startled for a second, but he stops when he sees me and speaks and is transformed from a ghost to a staff member in a lumberjack's red plaid shirt.

I knew very little of this before I stopped here, and it's a sobering tale of exploitation. At the Forest History Visitor Center, a more hopeful chapter is told. Films and exhibits tell of the lessons learned from the past and demonstrate today's forest management practices. Many thousands of acres of trees have been replanted that are now being carefully managed and harvested in sustainable ways. We cannot replace what is lost, but, thankfully, Nature is giving us another chance.

Encounters

The Great River Road between Grand Rapids and Palisade, Minnesota, stays close to the River, offers frequent access to it and has very little traffic – the perfect mix for a dawdler like me.

A deep indigo sky overhead shades to black in the west and gray melts into pale blue in the east as morning comes on. I drive slowly, taking side roads that beckon and then sensing my way back to the River. I doubt that I could feel any happier or more alive.

Ahead, the road is blocked for construction. A flag woman, bundled, hooded and red-cheeked in the coolness, gives me a bright smile. Her cheery, "Good morning!" sounds as if I might be her first visitor of the day and she is glad for the company. "How're ya doin'?" she asks, with a familiarity that seems not ingratiating, but endearing in a way that only a Minnesotan could pull off. As she explains the work being done, she notices the camera on the seat and asks about it, so I explain the journey of a raindrop and hand her a postcard. With that, she brightens even more and says, "Oh! I can't wait to share this with my nephew – he's a writer too!" So I give her another for him.

Then, in quick, animated bursts, punctuated with contagious laughter, she asks about places I will visit and she tells me about her nephew. When the truck arrives to lead me through the work site, she pats my car like a coach patting a player on the buns and says, "My name is Joan and I will be praying for you the whole way." In the rearview mirror, I see Joan waving and beaming, so I reach out the window and wave high in the air.

A few miles further, I pull onto what I think is a river access road, but turns out to be a private drive to a small house. As I am turning around, a loud and very unfriendly voice yells from somewhere nearby, "Can I help you!?" I see no one, so I yell into the air, "No thanks – just turning around," and drive on. The next road delivers me to the River and I walk down to have a look. Behind me then, a big pickup rumbles down the hill, spewing gravel and stops at an angle between me and my car. A red-faced, middle-aged man growls in that same unfriendly voice, "You were on my road. Why?"

In the next nanosecond, the details of the situation flash before me – woman alone, secluded road, burly, pissed-off man and big dog in truck blocking the ramp to my car, cell phone and pepper spray left in the car. Somehow, rather than inciting fear, that assessment of things brings a steely calm. I take a breath, stand up to every millimeter of my 5 feet 10 inches and look him square in the eyes. "I was looking for the river access and took the wrong road," I say levelly, and wait.

The moment hangs between us, suspended among alternatives, as he looks at me calculatingly. Then, like watching a shadow pass, his expression softens and he says, "Yeah. People do that all the time." So, I explain what I am doing, and he explains that he has had trouble with prowlers recently. When I tell him the story of the raindrop, he spends the next ten minutes giving me detailed directions to all the "don't miss" sites of his county.

When I give him a postcard he asks, "When will you arrive at the Gulf?" When I answer, "November 24th," he hands the card back and says, "Write that on the card, please." So I do – to which he says, "This will stay on my fridge to remind me to include you in my prayers every day until then."

It's barely 7:30 a.m. and two people have blessed the journey with their prayers.

Down the road a bit, on a one-lane gravel road somewhere near Palisade, I come upon a scene in a pasture that stops me. A woman and two horses are playing with each other – like you might play with your dogs. She dodges and bumps them and they push and nudge her, she runs a few steps, then swirls and heads the other direction like a football player with the ball and they thunder after her. When she sees me watching, she comes to the fence with both horses right behind her. I introduce myself and she says, "Come on in – they love company."

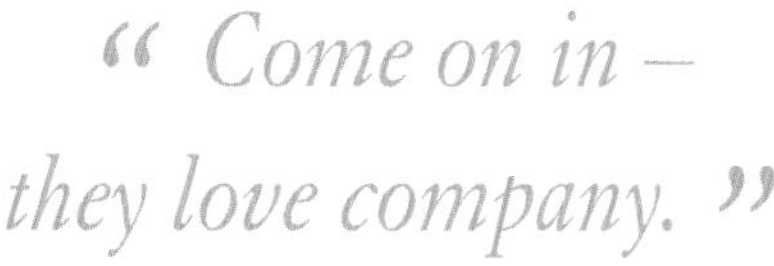

As the horses sniff me curiously, she introduces them as Tanner and Musta (pronounced *MOOsta*) and herself as Lisa Aragon. "They aren't 'rideable', just big spoiled pets," she says as they push each other away and nudge her for more affection. They give her big, slobbery smooches on her chin and cheeks with protruded rubbery lips and tug at her hair with their teeth. She comes every day just to play with them, she tells me, as she strokes and kisses their long noses and scratches their ears.

"Tanner is pretty easy-going," she says, nuzzling him, and then is nearly bumped off her feet by Musta. "But this one," she says as she laughs and grabs him by the cheeks, "deserves his name!" Lisa is Ojibwe, she explains, and "Musta" is a word that means "strong-willed one." "That," I say, laughing, "would have been a good name for my daughter. Then again," I continue, "I suppose my Mom would say the same about me."

As the three of them romp, I dance around them, shooting photos, laughing and trying not to be trampled. Then, Lisa and I hug and exchange contact information and the horses bump me gently as I scratch their ears and I roll on.

Such is the magic of a morning on the Great River Road.

The Storm

Life at the pace of the Mississippi River…

On day 10, the River is 265 miles from its headwaters. Since the average travel distance of our raindrop is about 27 miles per day, I am right on schedule.

I stayed home today to attend to the image processing, information organizing and logistics required to support this journey. Home, for now, is a simple fishermen's cabin on Lake Waukanabo, near Palisade, Minnesota. The small resort has no other guests and the lake has no public access, so it is exquisitely quiet. The resort owner kindly asked her son to extend the reach of their Wi-Fi before I arrived and she dug around and found a key for the front door when I asked, although her expression said that was a little silly. Abby, the resident Golden Retriever sleeps on my porch and is always ready for a walk. Last night at dusk, the achingly beautiful cry of loons echoed across the lake.

I was lured from my work twice today by the lake mirroring wispy clouds in a brilliant September sky. The crisp air sparkled and the pine-scented breeze was the perfect skin temperature as Abby and I had a walk. Now, I am on my front porch, watching the last of the blue sky be swallowed up by billowing dark layers of ominous clouds. I've watched the lake turn from glassy azure to dull slate to nearly black and dotted with whitecaps. A fisherman is racing for home as fast as his small motor will propel him, the sound of its desperate puttering muffled by the dense clouds. Somewhere, a dog barks urgently, wanting shelter. Abby has gone home.

The advancing, surging mass of storm cloud has dark underbellies and boiling white tops. It swells, then folds in on itself and then bulges out again heavier and even blacker. Goosebumps rise on my arms as the temperature dives – I hurry inside for my jacket and recorder. I can smell the rain now and see it at the horizon, but the air around me is still and empty, the energy sucked out of it by the power amassing above. I pull my chair closer to the cabin, turn on the recorder and wait – it's like the moment when the symphony conductor raises the baton and the audience holds its collective breath.

I think I can hear the wind coming. The first deep rumblings of faraway thunder roll over the lake and the clouds congeal to seal off the last bit of sunlight. Abruptly, the wind swoops in, raising dust on the road and swirling the trees like a blender. It turns colder and even darker. A sharp crack of blue lightning makes me jump and the long, bass drum roll of its thunder brings a shiver. A wall of rain is sweeping across the lake.

"…the air around me is still and empty, the energy sucked out of it by the power amassing above."

Day 10 Palisade, Minnesota *September 2*

The first huge drop hits the porch and, in the next second, the great clouds are unzipped. The lake disappears – there is no sky, no road, nothing but gray torrents of rain. I put up the hood on my rain jacket and pull back flat against the cabin, but the narrow eaves offer little shelter, so I open the door and set my chair just inside. I am spellbound, a captive audience. A bolt of lightning cracks so close and loud that it makes me yelp like a puppy and I chuckle, knowing the recorder has captured that as well. The next blast seems to rise up from the ground, making the porch tremble and the porch light rattle.

It's cold now, so I wrap myself in a blanket, but I stay in the doorway, awed, entranced by the storm's fierce majesty, thrilled by its dominion over everything until, finally, it begins to wane.

I am spent. The rain is now soft and steady as I get into bed. The sleep that claims me instantly is silky and luxurious, like that of a soothed and satiated lover.

Chapter Two: The Wild Child

"Moments like this are luminous pearls that shine forever in the heart of every traveler… "

– Gayle Harper

The Mansion

"You have arrived at your destination," says the GPS. Really? Wow! A park-like lawn reaches out from not one, but two huge mansions – one green and one white. I troll my memory to see what I know about the place and find…not much. When the invitation came to stay at Linden Hill in Little Falls, Minnesota, I simply said, "Yes, thank you." I remember having a quick glance at the website and assuming that it was a B&B in a lovely old home.

Inside the green mansion, a staff member and a volunteer docent welcome me and offer a tour and the intriguing story of the homes begins to unfold. In 1891, a pair of young bachelors, Charles Weyerhaeuser and R.D. Musser, best friends and each an heir to his father's lumber empire, began simultaneous construction of the two grand homes. Within a few years, each had found brides and began raising families in their elegant mansions overlooking the Mississippi River. The two families, they tell me, were all very close friends (which strikes me as fortunate since the homes are barely 30 feet apart)!

When the lumber boom ended, the Weyerhaeusers decided to follow their business elsewhere, so in 1920 they sold their home to the Mussers for a nickel and a handshake. Eventually, Laura Jane Musser became the sole surviving heir to Linden Hill, where she lived until her death in 1989, when she left both homes to the city of Little Falls.

We complete our tour of the green mansion and are walking to the white one as the docent casually says, "The lock on the front door is a bit tricky – you will find the side door easier." I find that a little curious, but I follow her into the kitchen. There, she opens cupboards to show me dishes and cooking pots and linens. Now, I am confused. She leads me through the dining room, the music room, a lovely glassed-in room called the "River Porch" and the library, where she says, "You are welcome to read any of the books. Just make

yourself at home." My confusion deepens. "Are there other guests?" I ask. "No," she says lightly, "this is your house for the weekend." ***What??***

I stare at her, dumbfounded, unable to formulate another question. "Feel free to cook your meals and explore the house and grounds. Just enjoy yourself." Although my mouth must be gaping open, I am still speechless, so I follow her up the stairs. "This was Laura Jane's room as a child," she says, "and you are welcome to sleep here if you like." Finally, I stammer out, "Is this a B&B?" "Oh no," comes the answer. "The home is used only for tours, weddings and special events."

"I watch the ripples reflect the changing light and I feel the familiar shift into a space of wonder and appreciation."

It is sinking in…it's me, alone, in this 30-room mansion. "Actually," she says, handing me a key, "since this is the start of the Labor Day weekend, we will all be leaving as soon as possible. You can just put the key in the drop box when you leave. Do you have any questions?"

Uuhhhh…

OK, I can't resist…"Is it haunted?" Her smile tells me she has been asked that before. "No," she says, "but I will leave you my cell number in case you feel nervous."

It all happens quickly. They are gone and I am left standing in a very quiet mansion, wondering what to do next. Timidly, feeling a bit like a trespasser, I wander through three stories of elegantly furnished rooms. I call my husband, my mom and my daughter – partly to share this news and partly because it seems so surreal that a little reality check might be in order.

I settle into Laura Jane's room, scavenge in my food box for dinner ingredients and then walk down to the River. It is serene and deep blue in the late afternoon light. A great blue heron stands motionless on a low branch, watching the surface for signs of supper. I watch the ripples reflect the changing light and I feel the familiar shift into a space of wonder and appreciation.

I select china and flatware and placemat from the array of choices and set a place on the River Porch. As I serve myself dinner, the last of the daylight through the trees paints long stripes across the lawn. Then, with surprising suddenness, it is dark and the house around me seems immense.

I'm not really nervous, I tell myself, but I will do my dishes quickly and go to Laura Jane's cozy room. The sound of my footsteps on the stairs seems absurdly loud and the hallway seems outrageously long with too many open doors, so I close them as I pass by.

I get in bed and pretend to read, but mostly I am listening. There is nothing at all to hear – no creaks, bumps or groans – and there is no sense of any other presence. There is nothing to fear except my imagination.

The yard light glows through lacy white curtains and softly illumines the sweet child's room. The house is deeply still. As the quiet becomes familiar, I relax and drift. Tomorrow, I will learn more about Laura Jane's long life in her home. Tonight I will sleep surrounded by her little-girl dreams.

Flying Dreams

Last night, in Laura Jane Musser's childhood bedroom, as I watched sleep edge in like the tide, I wondered if she had been friends with Charles Lindbergh. Surely they knew each other – growing up in the same era in the small city of Little Falls. It turns out that Laura Jane would have been 11 years old when Lindbergh, just 25 himself, rocked the world with the first transatlantic flight in 1927. I imagine her holding her breath, huddled around a radio with her family and then dancing and shrieking with joy when Lindbergh landed in Paris, knowing that a hometown boy had done something no one will ever forget.

Those early fliers have always been heroes of mine – their stories resurfacing in my life like their fragile little planes popping in and out of the clouds. Amelia Earhart was my childhood idol – my cat (who turned out to be timid and decidedly not adventurous) was named for her. My perennial answer to the grade school essay question, asking what person from history I would like to meet, was always, "Amelia Earhart." Because I have always had occasional dreams in which I could fly, I was sure that my hero had too – and that she had simply set about finding a way to recreate that in her life.

There was a time in the mid-1970s, when I suddenly found myself single with a small child to raise and felt lost in uncertainty. A friend introduced me to Anne Morrow Lindbergh, an early pilot herself and Charles Lindbergh's wife, by giving me her book, "A Gift From the Sea." I found such encouragement and

" The Mississippi River… how it has wound in and out through my life like the seasons! "

inspiration there that, over the years, I have given the book to at least a dozen other friends.

Then there's the photo assignment I once had in Amelia Earhart's hometown of Atchison, Kansas, on the 100th anniversary of her birth. There I met Fay Gillis Wells, a friend of Amelia's who became a dear friend of mine. Fay, a pioneer of aviation and an adventurer extraordinaire, had co-founded with Earhart the Ninety-Nines, an international organization of women pilots that continues to thrive today.

By the end of our photo shoot, I was so enthralled with Fay, who was a youthful 89 at the time, that I cancelled my plans for the rest of that afternoon. Instead, I spent 3 ½ hours with Fay at a fast food restaurant,

drinking lousy coffee and gobbling up tales of her wondrous life, while creating a treasured friendship. The following year, her son invited my husband and me to her surprise 90th birthday party in Washington, D.C. Along with a hundred other admirers, including some of great fame, we watched Fay bring down the house with a poised and witty impromptu speech and then work the room with grace and charm. Fay passed at the age of 94, but she continues to inspire me.

So, when I arrive at the Charles Lindbergh Boyhood Home on the outskirts of Little Falls, it feels familiar, like visiting the home of a friend. It seems that, if he were here, I would introduce myself and say that we have some friends in common.

It seems just right, then, that I enter through the kitchen door and find "Mrs. Lindbergh" there, peeling apples for a pie. "Have you seen that boy of mine?' she asks, "I have chores for him and I've no idea where he's gone off to now!" She clucks and shakes her head at the irrepressible spirit of her son, but her pride is obvious as she shows me the unheard of convenience of hot running water in her kitchen, thanks to a system that Charles devised. I didn't know until this moment, but today "just happens" to be Living History Day and the year being relived is 1918.

Out back, there is a shiny 1916 Saxon, still running perfectly, that Charles had dismantled and reassembled in order to teach himself auto mechanics. Then, at the age of 14, he strapped the family's luggage to the running board and took his mother, his uncle and the family dog on a road trip. Forty days and 1,900 miles later, after many roadside repairs, they arrived in California.

Across the yard from the home is the excellent Minnesota Historical Society's Lindbergh Museum, which has everything one would expect and much more. You can step into the cramped space of a simulated cockpit of the Spirit of St. Louis and try navigating it, and you can decide for yourself what to leave behind to cut the weight. There's original film footage and newspaper accounts of his transatlantic flight and of his lifetime of adventures. There are pictures of him at every age, but what never changes is the intensity in his eyes – like a cat about to pounce, he seems always poised to leap from some precipice into the unknown.

Still, it's the lesser known stories that capture me – like the account of meeting and falling in love with Anne Morrow while on a goodwill flight to Mexico, then teaching her to fly so that they could see the world together from this new perspective. I absolutely love seeing his road trip vehicle – a 1959 Volkswagen Beetle, in which he slept more than 100 nights by removing and reversing the seats to create a "comfortable, full-length bed." He traveled many thousands of miles this way, across the U.S., throughout Europe and, my personal favorite, following the Nile River through Egypt and much of Africa. In 1970, after coming in the Beetle to Little Falls, he was called away suddenly, so he left it for the museum, still packed for the journey with canned goods, air mattress, toolkit, machete and his canteen.

Things come full circle for me when I find this quote that shows how the Mississippi River lived in Charles Lindbergh and never left him, even on that long, history-making flight across the Atlantic. "The Mississippi River," he said, "how it has wound in and out through my life like the seasons! I grew up on its banks, swam through its rapids, portaged its headwaters with my father... I've barnstormed through its valley. Each flight on my mail route took me over its junction with the muddy Missouri. Now, the movement of the ocean waves below, extending on to the straight line of the horizon, reminds me of the river's wheat fields."

So, after several hours of being immersed in Lindbergh's exuberant life, it seems that I have met Charles Lindbergh, and that the meeting was arranged by my old friends Amelia, Anne and Fay.

Chickens and Polka

A banner at the edge of town yanks me from my road-induced stupor – "St. Stephen Parish Festival," it proclaims. I can see the church spire from here, beckoning like a compass needle.

In the church yard, teams of men are unloading tables and setting up tents. Women are arriving with pies, cinnamon bread and homemade doughnuts for the bake sale and laundry baskets filled with wrapped prizes for the Bingo game. A steady stream of pickup trucks is being unloaded for the auction. There's a nearly life-sized Christmas nativity camel, an apple crate filled with tools, fishing gear, a stationary bike, window blinds and a target-practice deer peppered with holes. People greet me as they work, not with one of those "held-back-a-little-because-I-don't-know-you" smiles, but with the big, jovial, wide-open smiles that seem to be the way of so many Minnesotans.

Something smells fabulous! I follow my nose into the church basement and find a small army of women in flour-coated aprons frying up 80-gazillion

Day 13 St. Stephen, Minnesota *September 5*

chickens and peeling mountains of potatoes. If they find it strange that I would wander into their midst, they don't show it for a second. When I tell them what I am up to, several immediately dust off their hands and invite me to sit down for coffee while they send for a neighbor who is their "best historian." She arrives in minutes, bringing a book of church history. Then, in animated, tag-team fashion, the women tell me about their village, their church and their Slovenian heritage.

The village of St. Stephen, which has been anchored by the St. Stephen Catholic Church since 1871, is the oldest Slovenian settlement in the United States. Slovenia, which is bordered by Italy and Croatia and tucked between the Alps and the Mediterranean Sea, was not a sovereign nation until 1991, but it has always maintained a strong cultural identity. Many of today's 870 residents of the town are descended from the first hardy settlers who carved their homesteads out of what was then densely forested land.

By passing on their traditional recipes and customs, by observing feast days and by throwing this annual party, tomorrow's Parish Festival, they have kept much of their rich heritage intact. By the time I leave them, the ladies have convinced me that I must come back tomorrow for a fried chicken dinner, games, cold beer and Polka music.

Five thousand people are expected for the Festival and it seems most of them must already be here when I arrive. The parking lot overflowed long ago and the streets of town are solidly lined with vehicles. I can hear the Oom-pah-pahs of the Polka band and the auctioneer's breathless stream of commingled words from four blocks away.

It's like one big family reunion, with everyone greeting, hugging and exclaiming over how much the kids have grown. The band is set up in a semi-trailer with one side removed and the musicians are a jolly lot. They tease each other, call out to people passing by and chortle when I point my camera at them. There are not many dancers yet, but there is much dipping and swaying of heads – even the cake walkers gently bounce to the beat. There is plenty of beer and a booth selling "Bouja," a harvest stew traditionally made with wild game, but cooked with chicken or beef for the Festival. There's a Heritage Booth, where a woman in traditional Slovenian dress is quizzing kids on their homeland – not many know the answers, but everyone wins a prize. I buy a raffle ticket for a gorgeous hand-stitched quilt, but I pass on the live goat, for fear of winning.

I join a long line of hungry people bent on chicken dinners and by the time I slide in at an almost-full table with my heaping plate, I've laughed and swapped

"I buy a raffle ticket for a gorgeous hand-stitched quilt, but I pass on the live goat, for fear of winning."

tales with a half-dozen people. Within four minutes, my table companions know my story and they begin telling theirs. They goad one another into "telling the one about…" and then fill in names and details when the narrator falters. It's boisterous and happy, like Thanksgiving dinner, complete with the sweet aunts, the jokester uncles, the rambunctious cousins and the adoring grandma.

Finally, stuffed with food that lived up to its promise and warmed to the core by the inclusiveness, the sheer "bigness" of spirit in this small community, I roll on, filled to the brim by the whole experience.

?

By flowing northeast from its headwaters, then looping eastward and finally southward, the Mississippi River has drawn a 420-mile question mark through the heart of Minnesota. At the base of the question mark, the stretch between Little Falls and St. Cloud, the River is leaving behind its babyhood, even its childhood, and is on the brink of growing up.

On this 14th day of the journey, the River looks and feels like the pack of 14-ish year old track stars that just ran by – lithe, high-spirited, sinewy and brimming with potential. The agile, strong, young River has not been dredged, channeled or girdled in by levees. It is still more blue than brown, still lined primarily with trees and uninhabited land and still described as "wild and scenic." There are no towboats muscling fettered rows of barges; only small fishing boats, canoes and kayaks keeping company with ducks, herons and bald eagles.

Change is coming and the River, like the boys, seems poised on a precipice where the freedoms of childhood will be replaced by the responsibilities of adulthood. Less than 70 miles downriver, at Upper St. Anthony Falls near Minneapolis, the first lock and dam on the River will make commercial traffic possible. Like a coming of age ritual, that will signal a change to a different kind of River. Right now, however, neither the River nor I have any weighty responsibilities.

This free-spirited wild child of a River calls people to be near it. Even the smallest towns along the Upper River have parks, walkways, benches and swings that are alive with people on these last glorious days of Indian Summer. At St. Cloud's elegant Munsinger Gardens, pathways etch the hillside like lace and the blossoms, now waning with the season, decorate it with muted beauty. I take up my place on a river bank swing and let the shimmering ripples of current mesmerize me until I melt like a cat in the sun.

In front of me, a trio of ducks as motionless as statues is arranged in perfect symmetry on half-submerged logs. As I watch, warm fingers of sunshine reach into

“Change is coming and the River, like the boys, seems poised on a precipice where the freedoms of childhood will be replaced by the responsibilities of adulthood.”

their shady harbor and rouse them. They shake, fluff and preen. Then, after one vigorous and synchronized shake of their tails, they plop into the current and glide away.

And, with that, it seems that a raindrop called Serendipity is drifting away as well. So, I stand up, resist the urge to shake my own tail, and set out to follow her.

A Little Fling

Minneapolis, the state's largest city, grew up along both banks of the Mississippi near the River's only waterfall, St. Anthony Falls. During the second half of the 19th century, as lumberjacks up north were filling the River with logs, sawmills sprang up near the natural power source of the falls. Even before the depletion of the forests brought an end to that era, however, Minneapolis had already turned its attention elsewhere – to the milling of flour.

By 1876, there were eighteen flour mills in the young city receiving grain from all across the Great Plains, and Minneapolis had found its new niche. In just two

decades, between 1870 and 1890, the city's population burgeoned from 13,000 to 165,000, as its flour milling industry grew to be the largest in the world.

Although indisputably lucrative, it turned out that the milling of flour was also dangerous. The fine flour dust created by the process is actually more explosive than gun powder. In 1878, a spark ignited the flour dust inside the Washburn Mill, which was then the largest in the world. A massive blast blew the roof several hundred feet into the air, demolished neighboring buildings and set off a raging fire that destroyed half the milling district. Today, the eerie ruins of the Washburn Mill still exist and are part of the fascinating Mill City Museum.

After that, the city's industry atrophied and dark days ensued. Mobsters began taking over at the end of the First World War until, by the 1920s, organized crime was so deeply entrenched that law enforcement was nearly powerless. Most officials had little choice but to either look the other way or to get on the payroll.

For decades, the Mill District was a lawless and scary place where unsavory characters roamed streets lined with crumbling, deserted buildings.

Then, yet another extraordinary metamorphosis began slowly in the 1970s and gained momentum in the 1990s, until today, the shady past of Minneapolis' Mill District is hard to imagine. My home here, the trendy, gleaming Aloft Hotel, is surrounded by shops, galleries and restaurants that, on this Friday evening, are packed with pre-theater patrons. Upwards of 35,000 city dwellers now live in lofts, apartments and condos in this vibrant neighborhood with a personality that blends urban sophistication and "Minnesota friendly." People on the street make eye contact and smile and, if I appear confused or stop to check my map, someone quickly asks if I need help. Real conversations happen in unlikely places at unexpected moments, with people of all ages. I'm falling more in love with Minneapolis every minute.

"Not only is the sweeping view breathtaking, but the mirrored surfaces divide and reflect the scene like a kaleidoscope"

In the morning, I begin with the magnificent Guthrie Theater, the centerpiece of the Mill District. Besides its full calendar of top-flight performances and several renowned restaurants, the building itself is an architectural wonder. When I glance up to see window washers on their trapezes against the blue, mirrored exterior of the building, I point my camera at them. One of the men notices me and gets the attention of the other and they pause in their work, grin and wave down at me as I shoot. Either Minneapolis is the happiest city I've ever encountered or it's my good fortune to cross paths with the happiest of its citizens!

Protruding from the back side of the Guthrie, overlooking St. Anthony Falls and the iconic Stone Arch Bridge, is the 178-foot cantilevered lobby known as the Endless Bridge. Not only is the sweeping view breathtaking from the open-air deck, but the mirrored surfaces on all sides divide and reflect the scene like a kaleidoscope. Like a kid with a new toy, I play with the compositions, sandwiching the River in between the eye-popping blue sky and marshmallow clouds above and its twin image below.

There's music wafting on the breeze and in the mall area below, I can see the canopy tops and shoppers of the Mill City Farmer's Market, and I know my next stop. Amidst the gorgeous produce, the maple syrup, apple cider, heirloom seeds and pottery, are some stellar candidates for my lunch. Winning out over the Tibetan dumplings and the walleye sandwich, is the intriguing sweet potato taco. I take my prize and settle on a top step, with a primo view of the colorful people parade.

Half a dozen steps beneath me, a little strawberry blonde cutie in a red dress spins around to look at me, then waves and beams up a whole-body smile. When I smile and wave back, she springs to her feet, marches up the stairs and plops down beside me. Feeling no need for preliminaries, she pokes out a tiny foot and says, "See – I didn't wear my sandals because I wanted to wear my green shoes." Her Mom, who looked startled at first, is now watching us with amusement. "They are beautiful," I say and glance at Mom for permission to take a photo. She nods and smiles. "My name is Hazel," says my new friend with a decisive nod, as she carefully unfolds two fingers and holds them up, "and I am two years old!" Then, just in case I don't quite get it, she shows me two on the other hand as well and says emphatically, "See… Two!"

With that established, she scoots a little closer to me and we chat about the sweet potato tacos, which she and her Mom have just finished sharing. Then, she gives me a serene little Buddha-smile and quietly turns her attention to the procession of shoppers below us. And there we sit, just inches apart, sharing a sunny and companionable silence until her Mom calls up that it is time to go.

Moments like this are like luminous pearls that shine forever in the heart of every traveler, reminding us that innocence and open-heartedness see no boundaries. Shine on, little Hazel!

The rest of my time in Minneapolis feels like speed dating. I say yes to a flurry of opportunities offered by the Visitors Bureau and I have fun at full throttle. For three hours I am a "human on a stick," rolling around on a Segway with a knowledgeable guide and a great group of people. I ride the Minneapolis Queen paddle wheeler, and I hang out at an Oktoberfest, swapping tales with other wanderers and watching polka dancers in beer stein sunglasses stomp and swirl. I visit Minnehaha Park to see the creek of the same name tumble over a 53-foot waterfall before joining the Mississippi. And, of course, I visit the first lock and dam on the River and mark the River's transition into a bigger, more serious waterway.

OK, I admit to being infatuated with Minneapolis. I've never seen a metropolis with so many parks, green spaces and bike trails. The list of community and cultural events in the newspaper, at least at this time of year, is long and intriguing. It feels healthy, clean, open-minded and authentically friendly. I've also been around the block enough times to know that infatuation can make one blind to the less-than-wonderful, so I ask for opinions. What I hear are consistently positive descriptions of life in Minneapolis with an equally consistent caveat. "The winters," they say, "are long, dark and *brutal*." It turns out that the city has the dubious honor of being "the coldest metropolitan area in the U.S." by a wide margin, with an average of 23 days each winter of temps below zero. Yikes!

Happily, for my two days in the city, the weather has been glorious, and I leave with my golden impression of Minneapolis firmly intact.

The Downshift

The deep, earnest chugging of a towboat engine pulls my attention from my computer for the umpteenth time since I set up my traveling office two hours ago. I watch as the rippling reflection of downtown St. Paul is cleaved in two by the slow-moving assemblage of barges. I am on the upper deck of a 1946 towboat, retired after 30 years of hard work and then rescued after another 20 years of languishing in dry dock. Its current incarnation, as the handsome Covington Inn B&B, is my home while in St. Paul. Although it is certainly one of the most appealing places that I have so far assembled my office, it is not conducive to a high level of productivity.

So be it. It's a glorious afternoon. After flowing southward through Minneapolis, the River makes a U-turn and enters St. Paul, then splits and surrounds Harriet Island, where the Covington is docked. The island has been a city park for more than 100 years and its 1940s era stone pavilion is a tradition in many families for picnics, reunions and wedding receptions. At the moment, though, all is serene, as I watch the wake from the barge recede and the reflection of St. Paul's skyline reassemble itself on the River's surface.

St. Paul, which is commonly known as one of the "twin cities," was described to me by one lifelong resident as "more like a slightly reserved older brother." The city's personality, I am told, is "hard-working, no-nonsense and conscientious." I resolve, once again, to follow its lead and pay attention to my work. And for a while, I do.

I cannot resist. Even when there are gaps in the slow parade of barges and pleasure boats, my attention is captivated by the silent, unstoppable movement of the River itself. Ancient beyond imagining, and yet constantly brand new, this River stirs something inexpressible in me. Being in its presence opens a door to that ever-present and yet elusive silence that resides just beneath the cacophony of life.

When the sun disappears and the sky deepens to indigo, the city lights across the River create long,

"I marvel for the thousandth time how such a massive movement of water can feel so deeply still."

dancing ribbons of luminous gold and white that stretch from bank to bank, and I am jolted into action. When a delicate crescent moon floats above the bridge, I race from one vantage to another as the light changes, my photographer's heart thumping like a racehorse.

Finally, all work set aside, all gear stowed, bundled into two jackets and a blanket, I am quiet again and alone on the deck and give myself over completely to the sublime beauty before me. I marvel for the thousandth time how such a massive movement of water can feel so deeply still. I watch until I dissolve and there is only the River.

Below, in the "Mate's Quarters," I open the porthole to let in the rich, organic scent of the night river and snuggle beneath the quilts. I am contentment itself as the River rocks me to sleep.

Chapter Three: Coming of Age

"No man ever steps in the same river twice, for it is not the same river and he is not the same man."

– Heraclitus

Confluences

I shuffle, foggy-headed, to the window. It's raining and still absolutely dark. The hotel room smells faintly of last night's dinner of tuna and crackers. I worked until almost midnight, but, interestingly, it doesn't even cross my mind to get back in bed. The sun will be up in an hour and it is time to go. Forty minutes later, I am showered, packed, fortified with coffee and have my orange juice and hard-as-rock bagel from the hotel breakfast bar beside me.

I switch on the GPS with no route planned and no voice activated, just for the pleasure of watching it track me companionably. It's raining more tenderly now and, in the east, a rim of luminous gray nudges up the densely black sky. There is something intensely intimate about watching the world come awake, like the first smile of a sleepy lover. The wet road is a silver ribbon in the headlights, beckoning me onward. With the heater baking my toes and the cool, dense air laden with earthy scents rushing in the half-open window, it seems that all my senses are enlivened and appreciative.

Two farmers, clearly a father and son in their identical khaki overalls, are working in a circle of light in front of a barn, hooking up a tractor. It didn't occur to them to sleep in either. A breakfast club of turkey vultures, feasting on fresh road kill, glare at me and snatch one more bite before reluctantly lifting off at the last possible moment. A doe and twin fawns watch from a meadow, but do not bolt.

The road rises and deposits me onto a high iron bridge and something about the familiar rumble of it under my tires makes me smile. Beneath me is the confluence of the St. Croix and the Mississippi Rivers. Surprisingly, at least on this day and in this still muted light, the St. Croix appears browner and the Mississippi bluer. There is a line of demarcation at first, then a tentative swirling and blending, and then a gradual surrender of their separateness into one broadened Mississippi River.

For the first time since the headwaters, 681 miles back upriver, I am leaving the state of Minnesota. From this point onward, until deep in Louisiana, the River will be the boundary that separates two states.

The sunrise seems to have done an about-face. The timid rays of morning light that briefly poked through the sodden sky have vanished. The sky and River are now identical shades of metallic gray and a fine mist is falling. From a high bluff, I watch the muscled-up River and remember being present at its perpetual birth 21 days ago. Many times between here and the Gulf of Mexico, I will stand at the confluence of tributary rivers and watch as they fortify the Mississippi. Truly the aorta of our continent, the Mississippi system drains 41 percent of the land in the 48 contiguous states.

A few days ago, I stood on the Laurentian Divide, which, with apologies to my geography teachers, I admit that I did not know existed. The Laurentian is a continental divide that separates the flow of water from north to south, as the more familiar Great Continental Divide does from east to west. Water on the northern slope of the Laurentian ridge

> *"When we try to pick out anything by itself, we find it hitched to everything else in the Universe."*

is flowing toward Hudson Bay and ultimately into the Arctic Ocean. On the southern slope, it is coming to the Mississippi to be carried to the Gulf of Mexico.

The raindrop I am following is part of the elaborate and endless circulation of water in, around and through our planet. That system is, of course, part of other smaller and larger networks from sub-atomic quarks and leptons to the movements of the Universes. As John Muir once said, "When we try to pick out anything by itself, we find it hitched to everything else in the Universe." Being in the presence of this great River somehow offers glimpses into the exquisite perfection of all those connections and reminds me that everything, including me, is in its perfect place.

Back on the road, a question bubbles to the surface. What is this all about? I've been asked in various ways and different answers have been given, but the question has many levels. It's easy enough to say what it's not about. It's not just about paying homage to the River's greatness. It's certainly not just about collecting photographs, experiences or stories. It's not about the book. I let the question float and swirl as I drive, like the fog cloud that alternately gathers and disperses over the River.

The Wisconsin section of the Great River Road climbs steep, dramatic bluffs and then drops into fetching villages. At Pepin, the River widens into an expanse of magnificence known as Lake Pepin.

When I've traveled it before, I've found the shops, cafés, bakeries and people to be irresistible. This morning, with a promise to double back in different weather and a more gregarious mood, I watch it all roll by like a movie.

When I reach Bay City, the rain has stopped. Armed with a steaming mug of fresh coffee and a warm cranberry muffin, I take the laptop to a riverside picnic bench. The question still niggles at the edges of my mind and I wonder if an answer will appear on the screen.

A fishing pier is blanketed with seagulls, murmuring softly, fluttering and jostling one another. Something startles them into a great commotion and they arise in swirling, complaining pandemonium. They move to another dock just downstream and settle there, still fussing.

Then, three of the gulls come back, flying in close formation and pass just in front of me. They turn sharply upward, braiding their paths, and then soar out over the River. In a maneuver that takes my breath, they reverse direction in a heartbeat and rocket past me again. They spiral upward then, twisting and trading positions and then dive, in perfect synchronicity, just inches apart. Once more, they pull up sharply, streak out over the water and make one final, grand loop before disappearing around the bend. I am spellbound and a little envious. They are pure joy and grace, playing with the air simply because they can.

There it is. This trinity of aerial acrobats has delivered my answer. This journey is about honoring the gift of this moment, just as it is, simply because it is given. It is about setting down my box of preferences as to how things *should* be and appreciating how they *are*. It is about stopping the chatter in my mind at times and listening to what lies beneath. At those times, I am as free as those gulls, living the moment fully, with gratitude, simply because I can.

Gesundheit

Just at sunrise, the rain stops, so I hurry out to make a few shots of the sleeping Main Street of Hastings, Minnesota. Within minutes, a new legion of dark clouds ushers in a cold wind and the deluge resumes, chasing the tentative morning light into oblivion and me into my room.

Now, cozy in my nest, wrapped in two sweaters and a blanket, I watch the frenetic wind whip curtains of rain in every direction. The gutters spread into small rivers racing downhill on both sides of the street. It has the look of being a day-long event, for the fourth consecutive day.

So be it. I'm nursing a head cold, the likes of which I haven't experienced in years. I have a bag of just-picked-yesterday Honeycrisp apples, plenty of tea and a good internet connection. I will spend the day right here, in sweet surrender to the sovereignty of the weather and one tiny germ.

I can't see the River from here, but I wonder how this rain must be swelling it. As I set up the laptop, there is a Mark Twain quote about the raw power of the River that I try to recall. I do a search for it and then laugh out loud at what shows up. "The Autocrat of Russia possesses more power than any other man in the earth," Twain said, "but he cannot stop a sneeze."

When the River is in "average" flow, its silent power can seem understated. When I stood at the headwaters at Lake Itasca, the average flow of the Mississippi was 6 cubic feet per second. When I watched it tumble over St. Anthony Falls in Minneapolis, that average had grown to 12,000 cubic feet per second. By the time the River reaches New Orleans, 600,000 cubic feet of water each second will be rushing past in a River that will be 200 feet deep.

That brings to mind another famous Twain quote. "The Mississippi River will always have its own way; no engineering skill can persuade it to do otherwise..." In Twain's time and since, what we see is that, although the Mississippi has been greatly altered, it will always expand and contract in order to handle the water that is brought to it. Years of effort by brilliant minds and countless millions of dollars have been devoted to "taming" or "controlling" the great River, and ultimately, it is no more stoppable than a sneeze.

There is comfort in knowing one's place. We humans create great stress by presuming that we are in charge. I close the laptop, lay my stuffy, achy head down and let the rhapsody of the wind and rain take me away.

"The Mississippi River will always have its own way; no engineering skill can persuade it to do otherwise..."

Day 24 Hastings, Minnesota *September 16*

RAMSEY ST
NO BICYCLES OR SKATEBOARDS ON SIDEWALK
1857

The Power House

A smiling, but tired-looking cook hands me a Mickey Mouse pancake and a plate of eggs. He and other volunteers are nearing the end of their shift, having served breakfast to nearly 800 folks at the La Crescent, Minnesota, Lions Club Pancake Breakfast. I join my hosts, Joseph and Joan Francois at a table filled with their friends.

The first time I heard from a Chamber of Commerce in a Mississippi River community that someone had invited me to stay in their home, I was shocked. I had never dreamt that people would open their homes to a traveling stranger in this way. Joan and Joseph, however, did just that – as did Jim and Pat Rossman in Elk River, Minnesota, and half a dozen others in River towns yet to come. The Rossmans are even "passing me along" to other friends downriver. It's part of the camaraderie that connects River people everywhere.

My breakfast companions have suggestions for my time in La Crosse, Wisconsin, my next stop. One in particular, lands with such resonance that I am certain to end up there. The St. Rose Convent of La Crosse, they tell me, is the Mother House for the Franciscan Sisters of Perpetual Adoration. More than 130 years ago, the Sisters began a round-the-clock prayer vigil that continues unabated today. Even when a fire raged in 1923 and the west wing of the convent was destroyed, prayer continued uninterrupted in the chapel, which was untouched by the fire. I am intrigued.

As I park beside the Convent, I feel hesitant. Are they accustomed to guests, I wonder, or will my visit seem intrusive? I am not a Catholic and I won't know the protocol. As if in answer to these thoughts, a woman of late middle age appears, pedaling a no-speed bicycle up the sidewalk. Her perfectly erect posture and pleasant but purposeful expression make me think of Mary Poppins. She stops beside my car, dismounts and looks directly in at me, then smiles with such genuine warmth and invitation that my hesitation is banished. With a brisk, "very well then" sort of nod, she turns and disappears through an unmarked door of the Convent.

Inside, Sister Jolyce is summoned to be my tour guide. She is wearing a neck brace and, as she talks, I see quick winces of pain cross her face when she moves too enthusiastically. Just as quickly, though, the pain is dismissed and her expression returns to quiet joy shining through clear eyes. Something about her reminds me of my grandmother – there is playfulness just beneath her no-nonsense history lesson about the Mary of the Angels Chapel.

Although many of the symbols and icons of Catholicism are mysterious to me, there is nothing vague about the artistry of the Chapel. Towering columns support soaring arches and the red oak pews are carved with delicate roses. Along each wall and in the skylights are the most vibrantly colored and beautifully detailed stained glass windows that I have ever seen. Sister Jolyce tells me that the windows were shipped from the Royal Bavarian Art Institute of Munich, Germany, which must have been quite a feat in 1901-1906 when the Chapel was built. The main altar is of exquisite white Italian marble and has onyx pillars with mosaics of Venetian glass and mother of pearl. At its center is a small door, behind which, the Sister explains, is a chamber that opens to the back as well and houses the holy Eucharist.

Day 24 La Crescent, Minnesota to La Crosse, Wisconsin

September 18

"You are not the first. I have had men walk out with tears streaming."

"In back is the Chapel of Perpetual Adoration," Sister Jolyce says in a voice that commands my full attention, "and *that* is where prayer continues that began on August the 1st of 1878." She looks at me for a moment, letting that register, and then says, "Would you like to go in?" I didn't know to expect this and I feel a shiver. Yes, I would like that.

Photography is not allowed, she tells me, and silence, of course, is observed. "I will wait for you in the hallway," she says. "Take as long as you like." This chapel is small and simple, with a semi-circle of pews behind a row of four chairs facing the altar. Two people are seated there, silently praying. I move along the back of the room and immediately feel a surprisingly powerful sense of Presence. The intensity of what I feel startles me and I am even more taken aback when tears suddenly fill my eyes. I sit down, thinking to gather my composure, but the tears flow. I head for the door, but I am shaken and a bit embarrassed. Sister Jolyce smiles knowingly and says, "You are not the first. I have had men walk out with tears streaming." When I ask if I might return and sit for a while, she smiles again and says she will arrange for a visitor's pass.

A potent mix of feelings is churning in me as I walk back in alone. I take a knitted prayer shawl from a stack, wrap myself in it and sit

in the back row. Within seconds, the churning quiets and I fall into a deep meditation. After a while, I sense something and when I open my eyes, there are now four people seated in the front row. A clock chimes, they all rise and together, they softly speak a prayer. Two leave then, as the two new “adorers” take the center seats for a one-hour shift. I close my eyes and disappear again.

The next time I open my eyes, I realize that it has been 90 minutes since I sat down. Amazingly, I had questioned whether I would be able to stay at all without disturbing others. My cold has morphed into a sinus infection and I have been coughing and blowing my nose ceaselessly. Since I entered the chapel, I realize, I have been perfectly still, without even a sniffle. And, after days of feeling unremittingly chilled, I am deeply warmed. There is a sense of having been held and nurtured.

It is just Love, of course. Love doesn’t notice if one is a Catholic, a Buddhist or a skeptic and it is everywhere at all times for all of us. Still, after 132 years of constant prayer by this lineage of devoted Sisters, there is an unmistakable concentration of it here. I understand now why the Sisters refer to the Chapel of Perpetual Adoration as “The Power House.”

Captain Jack

My bones creak with the dampness as I clamber over slippery rocks and squish through mud that wants to keep my boots. The River, broader and faster than it was yesterday, smells densely fertile and is the color of milk chocolate. Clouds hang like a sagging drapery and sunrise is a non-event. A whole tree floats by, thirty feet long with its massive root system spreading ten feet above the surface. For more than a week, heavy rains have drenched the entire Upper Mississippi Valley and the swollen River is doing its job.

After spending the morning in Villa Louis, an elegant and surprisingly intact Victorian mansion in Prairie du Chien, Wisconsin, I cross the bridge to make a pass through the amiable town of Guttenberg, Iowa, with its eye-candy Main Street.

Effigy Mounds National Monument, in a ruggedly beautiful area just north of Guttenberg, is a fascinating and sacred spot I have been before that is drawing me back again. The on-again-off-again mist is on as I arrive, but I put on rain gear and go for a walk. The earthen mounds protected here were built by American Indian people between 800 and 1200 years ago. Some are burial sites, while others are believed to be ceremonial, but many mysteries remain.

Memories of my first visit arise as I walk. I found myself at the entrance a full hour before the park would open, surrounded by a ghostly, beautiful fog. As I sat staring at the locked gate and the "Closed" sign, wondering if I had any options, a park ranger pulled up behind me. In a glorious heartbeat, he let me in and I had an experience I will not forget.

The fog, which was so dense at first that shapes 20 feet away were barely discernible, seemed a visual representation of the secrets held here. The silence was so profound and alive that it stilled my thoughts and only a wordless awareness was present.

My plan for the afternoon was to take an eco-tour with the Mississippi Explorer Cruises. The weather and high water have nixed that idea and cruises for today are cancelled, so I'll see what the day brings. For now, I am perched on a rock, just being with this immensely powerful River, marveling at its mood, which is unlike any I have seen yet. I am reminded of a quote that I first heard from an orange-robed holy man in India, but that is actually attributed to Heraclitus, an ancient Greek philosopher. "No man ever steps in the same river twice," he said, "for it is not the same river and he is not the same man."

Sometimes, the constantly connected state of life today still catches me off-guard. One moment, I am adrift in cosmic soup, where no distinction exists between the heavy sky, the ancient River and me. In the next, my cell phone shatters the moment and I grab for it with a racing heart.

The caller is Captain Jack Libbey, owner of the Mississippi Explorer Cruises. He and his wife, Dixie, are taking a boat out on the River, regardless of the weather, to scout some backwater sloughs and I am invited to join them. I happily accept.

We meet at a landing on the Iowa side of the River under a still leaden, but, at least temporarily, dry sky.

Captain Jack guides the flat-bottomed boat away from the main channel and into a labyrinth of shallow, marshy streams. We weave among hillocks of tall grass and small islands so impenetrably thick with trees and underbrush that the edges rise from the water like solid walls. Duckweed grows profusely just beneath the surface and tangles in the propeller, so we back

"Twice each year, this route that stretches from the Arctic Circle to the Gulf of Mexico, is used by 40 percent of all North American shorebirds and waterfowl."

up occasionally to free it. It feels hushed and secret, as though civilization is very far away.

We are deep inside the 240,000-acre Upper Mississippi River National Wildlife and Fish Refuge, the longest river refuge in the continental U.S. It stretches along 261 miles of the Upper Mississippi and protects not only the bluffs and open pools of the River, but also the surrounding wetlands and hardwood forests, as a sanctuary for wildlife. There are resident populations of bald eagles, beaver, mink, fox, otter, muskrat, coyote and deer and 51 species of fish.

Captain Jack pulls an arrowhead plant from the river bottom and shows me the tuber at its base. "This is a favorite food of the Tundra Swans," he says. "If you come back in November, there will be as many as 25,000 at a time feeding right here." I once saw a few of these magnificent birds, with their long, graceful necks and 6-foot wing spans, from a distance and it was unforgettable – I can only imagine being surrounded by thousands. The Tundra Swans use their powerful legs and webbed feet, he explains, to loosen the mud around the root of the arrowhead, before dunking their heads to pull up their prize. Often, he tells me, there will also be many species of ducks nearby, feasting on the small bits of food stirred up by the Tundra Swans' rooting.

Yet, the ducks and the Tundra Swans are only a small contingent of the migration of an estimated eight million birds that travel the aerial superhighway known as the Mississippi Flyway. Twice each year, this route that stretches from the Arctic Circle to the Gulf of Mexico, is used by 40 percent of all North American shorebirds and waterfowl. They depend on this refuge to rest and feed and, each year, as more wetlands are drained for development, more forests are harvested and more pollution fouls the water, habitat like this becomes ever more critical.

In a quiet moment, when the three of us are each lost in our own silent appreciation of this watery wilderness, a sudden, raucous squawk shatters the air. With a powerful whoosh, a great blue heron that had been invisible in the marsh grass beside us, lifts off and then squawks again. The lanky bird stretches out, skims the water and then disappears into the trees. Captain Jack smiles at the startle and says, "There's a big rookery of great blues just around that bend – not the biggest, though – some can have 200 nests." It's estimated, he tells me, that there might be 1,500 nesting pairs of great blues living within the refuge.

We putter slowly, deeper into the jungle-like maze. I've lost all sense of direction and the soggy blanket of sky gives no clue, but Captain Jack navigates unerringly toward something he wants to show me. As we round a small and densely-wooded island, he points to the top of a towering tree. It's an eagle's nest, a composite of branches and twigs so massive that it's hard to imagine how it stays up there. He smiles at my astonishment and, in a voice a little hushed with appreciation, he explains, "Eagles will return to the same nest and add new material each year. This one probably weighs several hundred pounds." It touches me, knowing that he has seen this many times before, to hear in his voice a sense of wonder that matches my own.

"I've been on this River my whole life and it has given me the life of my dreams," he says. "I was a towboat captain for 30 years, working all the way from St. Paul down to New Orleans. It was a great life, although it can be tough at times," he says, with a sheepish little smile for Dixie. "You are away so much, you miss out on a lot," he says, as she nods in agreement, but returns his smile.

When the time came to retire, Captain Jack wasn't ready to give up the River and he wanted to give back to it, so the idea for Mississippi Explorer Cruises was born. "Most people," he says, "even if they live nearby, have no idea what lies beyond the levee *and* they have no way to access it." He knew that if people could experience this wilderness and learn about the diversity of life that thrives here, they would be more likely to find their own way to help preserve and protect it.

Now, the company operates a fleet of eight boats, specially designed for these shallow channels, that offer eco-tours from four different ports on the Upper River. The excursions might focus on wildlife or bird-watching, on aquatic plants or on River lore, but all of them teach visitors about the complexity of life that relies on this wilderness for survival.

The cold drizzle that has been on-and-off until now becomes a fine, steady rain. I've stashed the camera, and Dixie and I have snugged up our raingear. Captain Jack, still in his t-shirt, doesn't seem to notice. He is in his element – as much a part of this River and this wilderness as the great blue heron.

On the Third Day. . .

Sunshine is a distant memory. The only breaks from drippy, grey skies for two weeks have been periodic violent thunderstorms. Everything in my vehicle smells dank. Plus, my bag of tricks for dealing with a raging sinus infection while on the move is as depleted as yesterday's lunch bag. I give up. I've scored some antibiotics and I'm going to bed.

My room in the 155-year-old DeSoto House Hotel in Galena, Illinois, has tall windows overlooking Main Street. On the sidewalk below, a few umbrellas-with-legs scuttle from one canopy to the next, but most folks seem to be tucked up somewhere staying dry. I make hot tea, crank up the thermostat and burrow like a mole under a mound of blankets. I have 48 hours until my next move and I am hoping for a supernatural recovery.

I slide down into a netherworld as murky as the weather. Day and night, sleeping and waking and strange, fragmented dreams are an indistinguishable

Day 32 Galena, Illinois September 24

muddle as a fever waxes and wanes. Surfacing enough to eat an apple or drink water feels like being dredged reluctantly from the bottom of the River. Finally, I sleep like the dead.

It's the morning of the third day and, although not quite a miracle, I am much better. Two steaming mugs of black coffee, a long, hot shower and a plate of eggs and toast convince me that I can carry on.

Outside, not much has changed – a battleship gray sky stills weighs on the world like a lead apron. Then, startlingly, a slit in the clouds opens and delicate, golden rays wash the brick facades of Main Street. I burst into action and, fifteen minutes later, I've got a few shots that I'm pleased with but, more importantly, I am rejuvenated!

Galena understands resurrections. The town was born as a lead mining settlement in 1826, and in fact was named for the mineral galena, the natural form of lead sulfite. The enterprise was so successful that by 1845, Galena was producing 80 percent of the nation's lead and its population of 14,000 was greater than Chicago's at that time. It was widely predicted that Galena would become the greatest city in the Midwest.

By the 1860s, however, things changed drastically. Consumers wanted metals other than lead, and the steamships that were a lifeline for Galena gave way to railroads. Galena fell into a decline that would continue spiraling downward for nearly a century. By the 1950s, Main Street was sad and decrepit and, all over town, hundreds of historic structures were neglected and deteriorating.

In the 1960s, however, the same historic preservation movement that revived many Mississippi River towns came to Galena. Entrepreneurs, who understood the potential of these irreplaceable buildings, set about restoring them, and the community gradually came back to life. Today, Galena's gloriously restored historic district comprises 85 percent of the town and more than a million visitors come each year. Now, many of the architecturally significant homes are B&Bs and art galleries, and restaurants and shops flourish along Main Street.

Dark clouds close in again and the seemingly unstoppable faucet-in-the-sky reopens. The visible world shrinks again to a 20-foot radius around my car. I can't remember the last time I saw so much rain.

So be it. I feel as revitalized as Galena. I'll drive in the rain and crank up Mary Chapin Carpenter. There's a raindrop to keep up with.

"It was widely predicted that Galena would become the greatest city in the Midwest."

Sinsinawa

I'm on a nameless two-lane road that feels like it will eventually take me to the River when, suddenly, everything disappears in a mix of low-hanging cloud and dense fog. There is only whiteness and silence, as if the world has blinked out of existence. Two beams of light, snuffed out ten feet in front of me, this vehicle and I are all that remain. We drift on the curvy road, swaying like a ship on an invisible sea. My world is circumscribed and simplified and I am brought fully present.

The road suddenly straightens and turns abruptly upward. The surrounding opaqueness allows no point of reference and the effort of the engine is the only evidence of a long, long climb. Slowly, up and up, I'm leaning forward, eyes wide open, as if that will help me to see into the nothingness. It is a strange sensation, anticipating the summit at every moment and wondering if I might just sail off the top like a ski jump at some point.

Then, finally, there is a plateau and a curve and, as unexpectedly as I entered it, I am spewed from my cocoon into a world of clear air and keen-edged details. It's a shock and a little disorienting. Fog is not unusual near the River, especially at this time of year, but I've never experienced anything quite like this. I pull over and get out to look back. It is surreal, a wall of white cotton candy, an unambiguous curtain dividing formlessness from the startlingly sharp lines of trees and road. It looks impenetrable from here, like a portal has closed behind me and there could be no going back.

"There is only whiteness and silence, as if the world has blinked out of existence."

I haven't seen the River in a few days; my hiatus in Galena was several miles inland. When it appears, a broad ribbon of luminous silver, I smile hugely at the sight. After 33 days of keeping company with it, my heart still does a little leapfrog dance each time it reappears. I pull off at an overlook and watch a pair of bald eagles ride an updraft, spiraling up from the valley below with only a barely perceptible tilt of wings. In this moment, the world is so beautiful that it hurts.

When I pull out onto the road again, I unexpectedly turn back to the north. It's not a moment of disorientation, but without a second's forethought, it seems I am going to Sinsinawa, Wisconsin. All I know of Sinsinawa, aside from loving the lyrical sound of the name, is that it is the hilltop home of Dominican Catholic Sisters who reportedly bake very fine bread.

I drive the 30 or so miles without question, and with no sign of fog. Away from the River, the land flattens out and long, cultivated rows converge at the horizon. Sinsinawa Mound stands alone, rising suddenly above the surrounding table-top of farmland, and seems perfectly suited to be the home of Sisters pledged to a higher calling.

I see no one as I drive through the shady campus, and I'm not moved to seek anyone out or even to enter the chapel. When I come upon a broad hilltop cemetery, I stop and walk among the rows of simple, white headstones, reading the names of the Sisters and wondering about their lives.

Just beyond the cemetery, on a small rise, is a brick pattern of concentric circles, which I recognize as a labyrinth. A small sign invites everyone to walk the path to the center while silently praying or meditating. I do, and, with each smaller circle, I feel more profoundly centered. When I stand in the innermost circle, there is a sense of everything being perfectly right. I feel content, settled, refreshed and healthy and decide this must be what drew me here; my visit seems complete.

Just as I reach my car, someone calls, "Come over here, will you, and help me a moment." It's a voice your mother might have used, or your third grade teacher – respectfully assuming that you will, of course, come immediately and do the right thing. The voice comes from a petite woman with curly gray hair who says, matter-of-factly, "This bench has blown over in the wind and we must set it upright." When our chore is finished, she beams up at me with sparkly eyes and an elfish grin and introduces herself as Sister Janette.

It turns out that while the Dominican Sisters of Sinsinawa are indeed bakers of bread, they are also bold activists who work to eliminate racism, human trafficking and anything that impinges on the basic dignity and rights of all persons. Since 1847, more than 3,200 courageous women have taken their vows at Sinsinawa before being sent out into the world to confront injustice and be a voice for positive change. They fearlessly take on human and environmental issues with nonviolent dissent and "faith-filled resistance" and have been doing so without fanfare for more than 160 years.

There is spunk, dauntlessness and a wellspring of warmth radiating from Sister Janette as she tells me about the community of Sisters and her job as the librarian. When I tell her about the journey of the raindrop, she is so delighted that it makes us both giggle. She asks about places I have visited and what lies ahead and she relishes every answer. She is, as my grandmother would have said, "just plain tickled with the whole idea." We talk and laugh like old friends, joyful to be catching up on each other's lives.

When I give Sister Janette a postcard of the journey, she looks at it for a long time. Finally, she looks up at me with eyes glowing and says, "You know, Gayle, today is my birthday. This card and this time with you is my birthday present." I give her a birthday hug then and, when I ask if I may take her photograph, her immediate answer is, "Yes, of course – if I can be holding the postcard."

So *this* is why I came to Sinsinawa – to help a friend celebrate her birthday!

Chapter Four: The Heartland's Open Hearts

"Here, surrounded by music and hearty laughter, watching innocence romp on the dance floor and warm openness across the table from me, I wish that I could share this moment with all who need it."

– Gayle Harper

Drifting Through the Driftless

I lean back, firmly feeling the rock wall behind me. There is enough room to stand comfortably on the ledge, but the precipitous drop in front of me is a bit dizzying. Although my backpack of camera gear feels as much a part of me as a camel's hump, its weight can sometimes throw off my balance. With an extra measure of caution, I remove it and set it beside me and then breathe in the expansive scene.

Far below, the River shape-shifts from wide and filled with a mosaic of forested islands on my right to a narrower channel crossed by a bridge away to my left. The glassy surface gives little hint of the volume of water moving beneath it. Train tracks trace the elegant curve of the River, the narrow bed perched between insurmountable crags and the water's edge. I bask in the driest air I have felt in weeks and relax, waiting for a train that will add color and movement to my photograph.

My thoughts wander to the work of the engineers who laid out the course of the tracks, letting the River do the heavy work of carving a passage through this rugged terrain and then following its lead. With that, a decade-old memory arises. While on assignment in New Zealand, photographing a group of affluent travelers, one evening's dinner conversation centered on a South African man who owned a road construction business. His most brilliant engineers, he said, acquiesced to the wisdom of the elephants when it was necessary to build a new road through the mountains. None of their complicated calculations had ever resulted in a better graded, more efficient route than simply following the elephant trail.

As the others exclaimed at the brilliance of nature's wisdom, I sat quietly, squirmy with discomfort. What about the elephants? Were they still using that trail? What was the effect on them to have their trail paved and opened to fast-moving vehicles? In my head, a debate raged between my conscience and my sense of propriety; I was the hired help among a group of the well-heeled who had paid dearly for this trip. Offending them would be unwise. In the end, I swallowed my questions like a hunk of dry bread. Now, as I envision myself nodding politely, an artificial half-smile stuck on my face, a fresh uneasiness arises.

Who knows? That same choice might be made if the scenario was replayed tonight and, realistically, it may have been no help to the elephants to speak up in that situation. Still, that memory, which has been stuffed in a corner with a "Do Not Touch" sticker for years, arises now for a purpose. It's an internal prod to stay honest and to use whatever voice I have on behalf of those without voices. We are all in this together, connected in ways we can barely discern.

I hear it before I see it; the wail of an approaching train stirs me into action. It snakes along the River bank, stretching so far that its head is swallowed by the trees below before its tail appears around the distant bend. I shoot frenetically as it passes and then sigh a big thank you to the young couple at the

Day 34 Savanna, Illinois *September 26*

convenience store who told me where to leave the trail to find this vantage point.

I am in the Mississippi Palisades State Park, on the Illinois side of the River, just north of Clinton, Iowa. For the past 120 or so miles, the River and I have traveled through a unique area of steep limestone bluffs and deeply carved valleys. This parcel of about 15,000 square miles, roughly from La Crosse, Wisconsin, to Dubuque, Iowa, is known as "The Driftless Area" and exists because of an ancient stroke of good luck.

Beginning around 1.8 million years ago, a series of ice ages brought great continental glaciers southward that ultimately covered much of the northern hemisphere. Somehow, each time the glaciers approached, a giant split occurred in the ice and this area was left untouched and completely surrounded by glacier. When the glaciers retreated, massive deposits of sand, silt, gravel and clay, known as glacial drift, were left behind, filling the valleys and leveling the terrain. The Driftless Area, having been spared that, is an archaic time capsule, preserving the rugged contours of the land as it was before the ice ages. There are even mini-ecosystems that are habitat for rare and endangered ice age life forms like the Iowa

"The Driftless Area is an archaic time capsule, preserving the rugged contours of the land as it was before the ice ages."

Pleistocene snail and the delicate spring-blooming Northern monkshood.

The Driftless Area is an enormous outdoor museum. You can, if you like, simply pass through and admire the limestone cliffs that sometimes tower 600 feet over the River valley. However, if you slow down and look deeper into the side canyons of ancient secrets and out to the densely wooded River islands, you might feel a connection to another millennium. The Mississippi has been carving this valley longer than my mind can grasp. I love knowing that it will continue, constantly changing and perpetually the same, far into the future. Seeing this lifetime as a pinprick on that continuum helps to keep "me and my stuff" in perspective.

I watch a tiny island, standing alone in an area of wide, swift current, turn golden in the last light of the day. High water from weeks of rain laps at the ankles of its trees. A turkey vulture glides by, just below me, its flight and the curve of its wing a lovely image of grace. When it circles higher, I catch a glimpse of its bald red head and ferocious beak designed for ripping flesh. We all have our niche, it reminds me. Each of us is designed for our exact spot on the web of life that stretches in all directions throughout time as well as space.

Pearl City

The Driftless Area ends with a thump. Without warning, the last of the rugged peaks are descended and the Great River Road plops me down into very different terrain. The pine-scented air gives way to the pungent smell of grain processing, and brown seas of shriveling cornstalks stretch to the horizon in every direction. Farmsteads dot the sea like green islands, an outline of trees enclosing house, garden, barn, silos and sheds. Along the River, configurations of tanks, smokestacks and pipes sprawl like giant tinker toys.

It's as if I've come through an invisible passageway and the transformation is so abrupt and complete that it leaves me feeling a bit flat-footed, so I take it to the River. Immediately, I am soothed and bolstered. The River and the land through which it passes may look different, but the River's silent, alive *essence* is always untouched by the superficial. Like a wise mother, it always makes me feel nurtured and then patted on the patooty and told to get on with it!

Relieved of my expectations, the moment is free to surprise me. As I roll into Muscatine, Iowa, a bit of wobble causes me to stop and check my tires. One is low, so I stop at a convenience store to ask where I might get it checked. The clerk tries to direct me, but gets confused, so another customer steps forward. "Why don't you just follow me," she says. "It's right on my way back to work." I thank her and, as we head for our cars, I give her a postcard as a small gesture of appreciation. She studies it and says brightly, "Well! I think you just need to follow me back to work!" It turns out that she works for the Muscatine Center for Non-Profits, which has recently established an Art Center. "Your project," she says, "is exactly the kind of thing we would like to let people know about." She gives me her card and I promise to come by when my tire is repaired.

"Between 40,000 and 60,000 tons of mussels were being hauled up from the river bottom each year and the beds were dwindling."

When I arrive, they are expecting me. I am introduced to Carlos Duran, the Artist in Residence and the organizer of the Art Center. As we tour the exhibits of talented local artists and Carlos' own wonderful paintings, we talk about the transcendent power of art and how it bridges differences in culture and language. Carlos, who is originally from Mexico, talks about his ever-changing art reflecting the changes in his life, and we laugh about the unpredictability of both. He invites me to return and mount an exhibit at the Art Center after my journey ends. Then he says, "Muscatine needs to know you are here. I am calling the newspaper right now."

So it happens that a nail in my tire leads to a visit from a journalist and a photographer at my B&B the next morning, an article in the *Muscatine Journal* the following day and an ongoing connection with Carlos and the vibrant art community of Muscatine.

Muscatine is plush with magnificent homes in historic neighborhoods. I wonder about the source of that wealth and when I learn the answers, I am reminded that there are no separate stories on this journey – it is always the River's story, just different threads of the tapestry. Remember the enormous logging industry that flourished in the Northwoods of Minnesota until the trees were depleted? When those logs were floated down the Mississippi, many came to Muscatine, where they were transformed into lumber, doors, window sashes and wealth for the mill owners.

In front of one colossal Edwardian-style home, a familiar name leaps off a small sign. The Laura Musser mansion, it says, is now home to the Muscatine Art Center. Remember Little Falls, Minnesota, where I was given the use of a 30-room mansion and invited to sleep in the room that was Laura Jane Musser's as a child? Curiosity pulls me inside, where a docent explains that Laura Musser of Muscatine was an aunt to Laura Jane Musser of Little Falls. They were quite close, I am told, and since both were musically gifted, they loved singing together. After my time in Laura Jane's home and bedroom, she feels like a friend, so when the docent starts up the giant antique music box known as a "Regina," it's a thrill to imagine my friend and her aunt making music in this elegant sitting room.

As we know, by early in the 20th century, the lumber boom was over. Muscatine, however, had already discovered a new way to prosper from the River's resources. John Boepple, an immigrant who had been a button maker in his native Germany, found that the shells of mussels that were abundant near Muscatine

could be made into lustrous pearl buttons. In 1891, amid much skepticism, he opened a small factory with a handful of employees, cutting buttons on foot-powered machines. The buttons quickly became the fashion rage, and Boepple's business transitioned into a two-story factory with steam-powered machines. More button factories quickly followed and before long another "Mississippi River gold rush" was underway. By 1908, there were 33 button factories in Muscatine, employing 5,000 people.

In the Button History Museum, I learn of the thousands of families who lived in makeshift riverside camps while fishing for mussels. The men, called "clammers," fished with a long rake, called a "crowfoot bar." The mussels, when touched with the crowfoot bar, would instinctively clamp onto it and could then be pulled into the boat. In the camps, women and children steamed them open in handmade cookers and searched inside, ever hopeful that they would come across that rare jackpot of a fine, valuable pearl. Then, the animals were discarded and the shells were sorted according to size and quality.

In town, other families had small cutting shops. The brittle shells required a one-week soak before cutting and the saws needed to be continually sprayed with water, so the work was wet and hard. As many button-sized "blanks" were cut from the shells as possible, but sometimes as little as 10 percent was usable, so alleys around town filled with great piles of "waster shells." The blanks were then delivered to a factory, where they were ground smooth, bored with thread holes, etched with designs, polished, sewn onto cards and finally shipped to market by steamboat or rail. At its zenith, Muscatine was supplying 37 percent of the country's buttons and the town was the indisputable "Pearl Button Capital of the World."

Great fortunes were made by the factory owners, but it could not last. Between 40,000 and 60,000 tons of mussels were being hauled up from the river bottom each year and the beds were dwindling. For a while, clammers tried working other rivers in other states to continue feeding the industry, but business faltered. By the 1920s and '30s, plastic became the material of choice for buttons, and zippers appeared on the fashion scene. The button boom was over.

I am sitting beside the River again, ending the day as it began, but this time in the shadow of a bronze clammer, perhaps modeled after an old photo like those in the Museum. He stands on a pile of mussels with his crowbars crossed above him, a no-nonsense look in his metal eyes. He is lean but strong-looking and has the air of a father willing to do whatever is necessary to feed his family. I wonder what they did when the mussels were gone.

In my palm is a button blank that someone gave me, cut from a mussel shell long ago. They can still be found along the riverbanks if one watches for them. One side is satiny and lustrous and the other is the coarsely lined outer shell, still embedded with river mud. I think about those who have touched it before me and all their stories, dreams and heartaches. I watch the shimmery surface of the River and try to imagine what lies beneath – are mussels growing there now? At one time, there were dozens of species of freshwater mussels thriving in the Mississippi. I know that some are now extinct and others are endangered as their habitat continues to be degraded by pollution.

The Mississippi River is a benevolent nurturer of life. It has no capacity to favor one use over another; it simply gives of its abundance to the mussels and the clammers, the trees and the loggers, the fish and the fishermen, and to all of us. It is up to us to use its gifts wisely.

Soul Songs

The graceful arches of the Centennial Bridge rise and fall above me as I cross from Rock Island, Illinois, into Davenport, Iowa. I drive as slowly as the morning traffic will allow, savoring the view of the River, which is now three-quarters of a mile wide.

I'm on my way to visit a friend, and memories of the day we met are as vivid as this impossibly blue October sky. A few summers ago, an unexpected opening in my schedule meant that I could squeeze in a River trip, so I faced the map of the Mississippi on my wall and waited for inspiration. The cluster of River towns in Illinois and Iowa known as the Quad Cities drew my attention and, when I discovered that the Mississippi Valley Blues Festival was scheduled soon, I made a few calls and started packing. Less than 48 hours later, I joined hundreds of music fans spread across the grass of Davenport's LeClaire Park in the sweltering heat of a Midwestern July day.

Day 39 Davenport, Iowa *October 1*

The River, as it passed alongside the park, seemed almost indistinguishable from the dense, humid air. The steamy music stirred us all into the haze so completely, we might have been inside a smoky blues club. People of all ages were melded into a single entity and we nodded and swayed to the beat as one.

Off to the side, couples were dancing, slithering against each other, eyes half-closed. A pack of boys had arranged themselves among the branches of a tree, watching girls doing cartwheels in the grass. People threaded the maze of blankets and lawn chairs, balancing cardboard trays of cold beers and spicy barbeque. It was all just right.

As I crouched in front of the stage, shooting close-ups of the musicians, the enormous speakers hammering the beat into me so that my heart reverberated with it, I felt light-headed and loose-limbed, even without any beer. When one band had sweated out their souls, recorded music filled in as stage hands prepped for the next one, so the sultry energy of it all was unbroken.

Blues music and the Mississippi River live inside one another. The sound was born in the cotton fields of the South, in the hearts of slaves, singing to sustain themselves and each other through their oppression. For those who managed to escape and find their way to freedom on the Underground Railroad, the route often followed the Mississippi River northward. Their music,

“Blues music and the Mississippi River live inside one another.”

of course, came with them. In the many decades since then, blues music has evolved and created sub-genres with increased complexity and differing techniques, but at its heart, it is still the sound of the indomitable human spirit, singing through adversity.

Longing for a few minutes of air conditioning, I decided to walk the few blocks to the historic Redstone Building and visit the River Music Experience. I knew of RME as a nonprofit entity devoted to preserving and nurturing America's music, particularly Mississippi River music, and I wanted to learn more. I found exhibits tracing the roots of American music, a coffee house with live entertainment and a full calendar of performances and classes for all ages. When I heard rock music reverberating from somewhere upstairs, I followed it to a performance hall and there, I saw my friend Ellis Kell for the first time.

A week of Rock Camp was culminating with performances by earnest young musicians playing for an audience of beaming family and friends. Ellis was at the center of a swirl of activity, shepherding kids and accepting hugs and handshakes from parents. I watched quietly; when he noticed me, he smiled as if we were already friends and gestured that he would be right there. As I have experienced many times, meeting a new friend along the River often feels more like discovering a pre-existing one. That's how it seemed with Ellis that day, and we have stayed in touch since then, so there was never any doubt that I would stop to see him on this visit.

Now, on this crisp October morning, we take mugs of coffee to a quiet corner and begin catching up on each other's lives. Ellis is a big teddy bear of a man with wise eyes, an easy smile and a heart full of music. A talented musician in his own right, he is also the Programming Director at RME. He talks about the power of music and its effects in his own life and the lives of those served by RME. He speaks of his daughter, Karli Rose, who died in a car accident at the age of seventeen and of the music scholarship that honors her memory. "It helps to channel some of the pain into something good for others," he says, "and you never know when the next Eric Clapton or Bonnie Raitt will appear. It just might be one of these kids who don't have the money to follow their dream."

Our conversation hopscotches its way right through lunch and, among the topics, there is this – Ellis and his wife, Kristi, recently enjoyed spending a night on a towboat as it pushed its load of barges on the Mississippi River. "*REALLY?*" I blurt, "My God, I have been trying to make that happen for years!" I have, in fact, hinted and asked outright nearly every person I have met who works with the barges about the possibility of getting on board. Inevitably, the answer has always been some version of, "Sorry, but security is so tight now that no one is allowed to come aboard except employees." Now, Ellis is looking at me with a little cat-swallowed-the-canary smile. "Well," he says quietly, "I just might be able to make that happen." I look back at him, wide-eyed, thrilled at the possibility, but not wanting to press. He knows what that would mean to me and to this project, so, although it takes a colossal effort, I say no more and will wait to see what unfolds.

When Ellis tells me that his acoustic trio – "The Whoozdads?" – will play tonight, I promise to show up. I'll have a two-hour drive to my next lodging at the end of the night, but the opportunity is too good to miss. The trio, composed of Ellis, Tony Hoeppner and Mike Frank, took their name from an overheard comment from a young person, "Whose dads are those?" They each bring so much talent and have such obvious fun playing together, and their mix of old favorites and original compositions is so engaging, it's hard to make myself leave. When I finally do head out on the dark road, the guys have loaded me up with new CDs, so the drive seems short and lively with their accompaniment.

It's all just right.

Forty Days and Nights

On this 40th day of keeping company with a raindrop, the Mississippi has traveled just over 950 miles from its headwaters and I have driven more than 3,500 miles in my wandering, looping way. Life has settled into a steady, unhurried rhythm, matching that of the River. The routine of living out of my car and moving every two days is easy and familiar. In 25 minutes, I can have the car unloaded, the computer downloading images and my road food dinner of microwaved soup, tuna, crackers, fruit and tea prepared.

The logistics of life have become simplified and streamlined. I've learned to carry a night light in my overnight bag so I can find the bathroom in the dark. I've learned, after giving a desk clerk an entertaining moment, to return both hotel key cards at checkout. I found myself locked out of my room one night, so I went to the front desk. "My key card," I said, "seems to have quit working." She looked at it and then at me and, with obvious effort, held back her laugh and said politely, "Ma'am, this card isn't from our hotel." I know she enjoyed telling that one.

I remember the morning I kissed Mike goodbye and let go of that last lingering embrace, knowing that it would be six weeks before the next one (he will come to meet me in another week). As I took to the highway, the doubts and fears that suddenly swarmed like mosquitoes caught me by surprise. Counting the trip to the headwaters and home from the mouth of the River, I would be alone on the road for 96 days. Even for a natural-born traveler, that's a long time. The journey had created itself so effortlessly that there had never been a second's hesitation. But, on that first morning, looking out at 96 days of the unknowable, I suddenly wondered what I had gotten myself into.

In the end, a well-worn memory arose, soothing and encouraging me, as it has for years. On my 30th birthday, I gifted myself with a week of sky diving lessons. We learned which cords to pull at which altitudes, but most importantly, we learned how to land. Each evening in class we jumped from progressively higher platforms, learning to hit the ground with a smooth, 4-point roll. The airplane we would jump from was double-winged and our instructions were to grab the diagonal strut firmly, step out onto the wing and wait for the jump master to slap your leg. When the slap comes, push hard, as if pushing the plane away from you. I had been through it in my mind a hundred times – I felt excited, prepared and fearless.

The big morning finally arrived and the weather was good. We went over the instructions one last time and suited up, and it turned out that I would be the first to go. I felt strong and confident. I grabbed the wing strut and stepped out onto the wing and into the most staggeringly intense wind I had ever experienced. Somehow, I had never considered how that wind would feel and it was like facing into a hurricane. In one second, my bravery was blown away and in its place was icy fear. I held on with a death grip as my mind *screeched* at me, "Gayle! What the *hell* are you doing?" Then, from somewhere deeper, I heard another voice that seemed to be mine and not mine at once. "You might as well jump now," it said. "You are standing on the wing of a plane." Then came the slap, the push and a thrilling, magnificent, never-to-be-forgotten experience.

In the years since then, that voice has spoken many times when uncertainty had me clinging to the edge of some figurative precipice. Each time it has lovingly booted me off into the unknown and I have never regretted it.

Day 40 Burlington and Montrose, Iowa *October 2*

Now, the last stars are fading into the 40th dawn, and the day is a gift to be unwrapped. As the light comes up and a thin veil of fog clears, the world recreates itself, and the shapes of rolling hills and tidy farms arise from the ether.

I know nothing about the town of Burlington, except that a few people have mentioned Snake Alley. Since I don't quite get what that is, I start there. It turns out to be a brick street, reminiscent of San Francisco's Lombard Street, that squiggles its way down a very steep hill. It was, when built in 1894, a creative way to provide more secure footing for horses negotiating the hill in snow and ice. It worked, it seems, at least on the downhill trek, but, after some serious uphill tumbles, the city fathers declared it should be a one-way street and so it remains today.

As I am getting my shots, there is a cheerful, "Good morning," from a woman walking her dog. In the unguarded, interested way of so many Iowans, she wants to know where I am from and what I am up to. I've come on the perfect day, she tells me, and I *must* stay for the Oktoberfest. I believe she is right.

Most folks in this southeast corner of Iowa are descended from the millions of German immigrants who came in the late 1800s to settle in the Midwest and along the Upper Mississippi River. So, when the local Lions Club throws a party with cold beer, bratwurst, sauerkraut, German potato salad and apple strudel – and it's all accompanied by a good polka band – hundreds will come to celebrate their heritage.

It's early afternoon when I arrive, but the beer is flowing and the band is playing. There aren't many grown-up dancers yet, so the floor is the domain of blonde, porcelain-skinned little girls twirling and stomping with joyous abandon. When the music slows to a ballad, they snuggle close, giggling and swaying dreamily and delighting their audience. When the band takes a break, a lederhosen-clad musician, dubbed "The Happy Bavarian," strolls through the crowd and into the food service area, where he disrupts everything by flirting with the help. Peals of laughter follow him.

People recognize me as being "not from here" and offer beer, food and conversation. Once again, I walked in a stranger and immediately feel welcomed and included. Much is said these days about loneliness and alienation being rampant in our society. Here, surrounded by music and hearty laughter, watching innocence romp on the dance floor and warm openness across the table from me, I wish that I could share this moment with all who need it.

I've been in this area before. I came to Montrose, Iowa, not long ago for the annual Watermelon Festival, where nine tons of free watermelons were served to thousands of neighbors. After the parade, the picnic, the seed-spitting contest and the chicken poop bingo, I left to scout for a sunrise view of the River. A woman I passed looked up from tending her flowers and smiled

"The floor is the domain of blonde, porcelain-skinned little girls twirling and stomping with joyous abandon."

and waved, so I stopped. Within five minutes, I was clearing the heap of maps, water bottles and travel paraphernalia from my front seat so she could climb in and take me to her favorite overlook.

That's how I met Peg, who later introduced me to her next-door neighbor, Rhoda, who invited us both for lemonade. After a few minutes of chatting on Rhoda's deck beside the River, she invited me to cancel my hotel reservation and stay in the small cabin next to

her home, promising that there was no better place on earth for sunrises. I did, of course, and was greeted at dawn with the vision of splendor that you see here.

Such marvelous encounters are not unusual. It might be tempting to attribute them to the trusting, good-natured character of people in the Heartland or to the powerful harmonizing effect that the Mississippi seems to have on us, but there is more to it.

If this journey and this book have a purpose, at least part of it is to allow the basic goodness of human nature to reveal itself. When we let down our guard, it shows up everywhere, shining like the sunrise.

Once Upon a Time...

The charms of the Great River Road are often subtle gems. For the most part, these River towns are not tourist destinations with billboards and attractions clamoring for your attention. Instead, you are invited, if you like, to slide into life as it is being lived. Then, in whatever way is natural, the place may begin to tell its stories. Before you know it, it can be like facing a full box of dark chocolates – eventually, one just has to be chosen. In Keokuk, I will choose two.

Keokuk is at the absolute end of Iowa. It is perched on the southern tip of a spit of land, shaped more like a cleat than a boot heel, that appears to have been chunked out of the state of Missouri by the course of the Des Moines River.

Although I was clueless until I arrived, it turns out that Keokuk is at the center of an area roughly 35 miles in every direction that is a mecca of sorts for rock hounds. For geologic reasons more complex than I can grasp or explain, geodes are found here in great abundance. The lumpy balls of sedimentary rock seem to bubble to the surface along creek beds and drainage ditches after every good rain. On the outside they look

something like a petrified cauliflower, but on the inside there are beautiful configurations of ancient crystals in a rainbow of colors.

The annual Keokuk Geode Fest, which took place just a week ago, brought 800 collectors from around the world. They foraged in the mud on private land, which was opened to them for this special event, and carried out buckets full of geodes. Although many are about the size of a grapefruit or smaller, a few can be as big as a beach ball. Part of the fun of the gathering is to have the geodes split open on the site so that everyone can share in the discovery and perhaps buy, sell or swap some treasures.

I'm staying across the River in Hamilton, Illinois, with my new (but already dear) friends, Vickey and Harold Henson. Upriver friends Jim and Pat Rossman, who graciously hosted me in Elk River, Minnesota, "passed me along" to the Henson's and, as predicted, it had taken me a solid three minutes to feel at home with them. This morning, after feasting on Vickey's fabulous cooking, they took me to their secret spot for geode hunting and, in less than an hour, our backpacks were loaded with all we could carry.

Now, Vickey and I are on a downtown Keokuk sidewalk watching Kirk Brandenberger, the Executive Director of the Tourism Bureau and somewhat of a rock hound himself, haul out the homemade geode-splitting contraption that he keeps in his office. In a practiced motion, Kirk wraps a heavy chain embedded with round blades around a geode, pushes down on the long lever, and the blades are squeezed into the rock. As it creaks with the pressure, Vickey cups her hands on both sides of the geode, ready to catch it. Then, with a resounding *crack*, it breaks in two. Vickey brings it to me, holding the two halves together and says solemnly, "You must be the first to see inside your geode – no one has seen this in 300 or 400 million years." Then, slowly, she separates them, and matching bowls of glowing amber crystals in concentric circles are revealed. In the center are sharp-edged pyramids of pure, brilliant white, gleaming in the sunlight for the very first time. It is exquisite.

Experienced geode collectors can tell by the weight which ones will have the more prized hollow centers, but I am intrigued by them all. Some are nearly filled with crystals and interlaced with tiny dark tunnels. They come in soft shades of rose, orange, gold, gray and blue and some are as clear as diamonds. Some I decide to leave whole, keeping their secrets intact a while longer. I'll send them home with Mike when he visits soon and make them part of a backyard art project I am imagining. Holding these relics of antiquity in my hands and watching the brilliant perfection that has been growing inside for eons sparkle in the light for the first time is thrilling. It leaves me feeling a bit hushed and reverent, as if I had visited a great museum and been allowed to touch!

The other story in Keokuk has a surprisingly personal twist. At the bottom of the hill below downtown, surrounded by a field of weeds, is the old railroad depot, long abandoned and boarded-up. Something about it calls me, so I high-step through the weeds, scattering grasshoppers and hoping that it's too chilly for snakes. It's an elegant structure, in spite of its decaying roof and years of neglect. No whistle-stop depot, it's nearly a half-block long and obviously had once been a grand hub of activity. I stand beneath the graceful arch of the iron portico, which is still perfectly erect, and imagine benches filled with travelers, suitcases at their feet.

" You must be the first to see inside your geode – no one has seen this in 300 or 400 million years. "

Slowly, gradually, a memory as dusty as my surroundings is wafting to the surface of my mind. I remember my Grandma Irma talking about Keokuk. I can hear her way of saying it, as if all one word, "Keokuk-Iowa-on-the-Mississippi-River." But, what had she said? I call my Mom. She remembers her speaking of it, too, but can recall no specifics. I call my Uncle Dale in Omaha. Yes, he remembers – and as I stand beside the silent tracks, he tells me.

My grandmother's parents had divorced when she was young, an unusual and scandalous event in the early 1900s. Her father remarried and settled with his new wife in Keokuk. As a girl, my grandmother had visited them, taking the train alone from Omaha to Keokuk. I stand very still and listen. Beneath the chattering insects and the drone of something industrial, there are echoes of lives. Countless tearful farewells and joyful reunions took place beneath this portico, watched silently through the windows by those just passing through. Among them had been my Grandma Irma, stepping from the train and scanning the crowd for her father's face.

I know she was a pretty young woman with dark, wavy hair and I think that she must always have carried herself with dignity. I imagine her in a long, high-collared dress with a brooch at her throat and a broad-brimmed traveling hat. I feel her – dusty from the journey and a bit weary, but excited to see her father and anxious about her new stepmother. I wonder how the visit went. Did they get along? What did she do while here? Did she hunt for geodes?

I know that my grandmother had dreams of being a writer. Did she write about this adventure? Was there a part of her standing aside, watching as she found her father, observing and recording it so she could later tell the tale? I wonder what she would have thought if she could know that, nearly a century later, her granddaughter would stand in her footsteps, trying to imagine her thoughts. In this moment, I see my grandmother as I never have before – not just as the character of "grandmother" in *my* story, but as a young woman with her own rich story of dreams and heartaches, who had no idea that I would ever exist.

Keokuk's stories have all transcended time. A friendship that already feels old has been created in two days. Crystals growing in a dark cocoon for millions of years caught the fire of daylight in my hands. And, my dead grandmother lives in my mind in a more whole way than ever. It's time to sit by the River and silently tell it these new tales.

The Phyllis

I don't remember if there was a barge on the Mississippi River when I first glimpsed it as a 9-year-old, but it does seem I have been fascinated with them for that long. The barges, like the trains that accompany the River, are part of the vast movement of energy that has always gathered around the Mississippi. Since long before there were trains or roadways, the River has always been the continent's superhighway for transporting goods and people.

Today, nearly 500 million tons of cargo are moved by barges on the Mississippi each year, and their presence is an integral part of any experience of the River. I have watched them and photographed them from the air, from bridges, from riverbanks and from the water, in all kinds of weather. I've stood waiting as a barge approached a turn in the River that I was certain would be too narrow and sharp, only to see it glide through without even changing pace. I've watched the

broad beam of a barge slide into a lock, with just a few feet of leeway on either side, with more ease than I parallel park my car. I've come to know the vibration that precedes the deep bass sound of the engine and can tell by the timbre if it is coming up or downstream. Dozens of times, I have hurried to some vantage point to watch the smooth, sedate passing of a barge and then waited for the waves from its wake to roll toward me in perfect rows. I have marveled, repeatedly, how something so enormous and cumbersome can seem to move with such grace.

I've seen captains silhouetted in their glass towers and deckhands walking nonchalantly along narrow ledges and wondered about their lives. I've waved and felt as pleased as a 7-year-old when they waved back, but I've never been able to get any closer. I've met lots of folks who work with the barges in various capacities and I've hinted and asked outright about the possibility of getting onboard and always been told that security prohibited it. I've also met lots of people who are at least as curious as I am about what it's like to live and work on the barges in what has been described as "the invisible industry," but mostly, they remain inaccessible and a little mysterious.

" Since long before there were trains or roadways, the River has always been the continent's superhighway for transporting goods and people. "

So, when my friend Ellis sat across the table from me last week in Davenport and flashed a quick grin as he said, "I think I might be able to make that happen for you," it felt as if he had just placed a lighted firecracker on the table between us. Since then, Ellis has contacted his good friend, Jeff Goldstein, who happens to be the CEO of Alter Barge Line, one of the most vital and respected companies in the industry and, amazingly, Jeff has given his permission – for more than I could have imagined. Tomorrow morning, an Alter Barge crew van will take me from Quincy, Illinois, to Clarksville, Missouri, where I will board The Phyllis, a towboat traveling upriver. I will be onboard for 24 hours, sleeping in the guest quarters, eating with the crew and experiencing life on a barge!

There is an early morning message that The Phyllis has been delayed by a heavy fog. In order to meet her, we will need to drive farther south than planned, to Winfield, Missouri, 100 miles by road from Quincy. That changes our schedule and makes it very tight. When Carol, an Alter Barge employee, arrives in the van, we are on our way in seconds. She drives as fast as

doors marked "Mate," "Cook," "Pilot" and "Captain" to the 3rd floor guest quarters.

I hadn't given a thought to what my accommodations might be like, but I would never have imagined this! There is a spacious sitting room with a large picture window looking out over the barges, an adjoining bedroom with another large window and a private bathroom. We leave my bag and take the last flight of stairs to the pilot house. Pilot Jeff Keller welcomes me heartily and then turns back to his array of controls and computers, as he is ready to move the barges out of the lock and back into the main channel. (We really did just make it in time!) I stand back and watch quietly, feeling a bit surreal that I am actually here.

Once underway, Jeff begins to orient me to their work and life on board. The term "towboat" is sometimes confused with "tugboat," but they are quite different. A towboat, which doesn't actually tow, but pushes its load, got its name in the early days of transporting goods by boat, when the power was provided by a draft animal towing the boat as it walked alongside a canal. A tugboat, which may push or pull its load, is much smaller and is used to move a barge in or out of a harbor, to deliver supplies or personnel to a towboat or to move larger vessels in places where navigation is difficult. The Phyllis, originally built in 1973, is an average-sized towboat, measuring 140 feet long by 42 feet wide. Her 6,000 horsepower engine uses 2,000 gallons of diesel per day and two semi loads of fuel are needed for a fill-up every ten days.

Here on the Upper Mississippi above St. Louis, towboats usually push the allowed maximum of fifteen

she can get by with and, thankfully, there is almost no traffic. We careen into the parking lot and run with my bags – The Phyllis is there, making her way through the lock.

A deckhand comes to meet me, and my overnight bag and camera case are passed down to him. He tosses a life jacket to me and, with it on, I climb down a narrow metal ladder built into the side of the lock and then step across the two-foot gap above the water onto the ledge of a barge. The smiling deckhand steadies me, then tells me to keep to the inside and follow him. My heart is pounding like a racehorse, and I must be grinning ridiculously, as we make our way along the outside of several barges, lashed together end to end.

When we finally step down onto the deck of the towboat, I can look up and around. It's much bigger than I expected – four stories tall at the bow, tapering to one at the stern, and gleaming white in the morning sun, with striking gold and black trim. I hear pride in the deckhand's voice as he tells me that she has just been freshly painted and completely refurbished. I follow him through a maze of halls and stairways, past barges, bound together three abreast and five long. Since each barge is almost 200 feet long by 35 feet wide, the entire load measures nearly 1,000 feet long by 105 wide. Barges are the most efficient way to transport heavy cargo like coal, grain or iron, as each individual barge can be filled with up to 1,500 tons. To give me a sense of that, Jeff tells me that it would take 58 large semi-trucks or 15 jumbo hopper railroad cars to carry the equivalent of each barge. That means it would take 870 tractor trailers, which when strung together would stretch for 35 miles, to carry the load now being pushed by The Phyllis. As Jeff adjusts the levers and taps the joystick from side to side to maneuver the boat, he also tells me about the system of channel markers used for navigation and the radar and weather systems that he continually monitors.

No area is off-limits, he says, and I am free to wander the boat and talk with anyone. There are eleven crew members, alternating six-hour shifts around the clock, and everyone works 30 days on and 30 off. As Pilot, Jeff alternates shifts at the helm with Captain Ross Marcks. "There's the Captain now," he says, "out for his morning exercise before he comes on duty." Four stories below, I can see him in his life jacket striding along between the barges, stepping easily over the cables holding them together without breaking stride.

He loops around the far end and begins again. "It's a challenge to stay in shape," Jeff says, "plus the food is good and is always available. Most of us put on weight."

When I set off to explore, the first person I meet is Marilyn, the cook responsible for all that good food. She is stirring a few pots that smell fantastic, doing dishes and checking on chocolate chip cookies in the oven. "Somebody's always hungry," she says in a voice that sounds like the mother of teenagers, "although sometimes I think they just eat out of boredom." When she can take a break, we sit with a cup of coffee and she tells me about her life on the boat. She orders her groceries by fax and they are delivered by a "boat store" every ten days or so. Delivery day is eagerly anticipated because it also brings a fresh newspaper to replace the tattered and splattered one they have all read several times. They do have a small lounge with satellite TV that helps them feel less isolated. "That's the hardest part," she says. "It's a good job, but I do get lonesome for my home and family."

Throughout the afternoon, as I meet other crew members, I hear that several times. "Life goes on at home without you," one tells me. "There are births, graduations and funerals and you aren't there for them. And, when something goes wrong and you aren't there to help, it's really tough on everyone." When I talk with Captain Marcks, he says, "It's not the life for everyone – people either love it or hate it." About his crew he says, "We are a lot like family and we live in very close quarters, so sometimes there are squabbles. Mostly, though, it's a good and peaceful life." Then he waves his hand at the expanse of windows around him and says, "Besides, look at the view I enjoy every day."

I spend some time out on the front deck taking in that view, which is very different for me. Instead of stitching together a picture of the River from disparate access roads, the whole of it is experienced, each alluring curve revealing its own wonders as we round it. With only occasional glimpses of civilization, it feels mostly wild and natural.

Nothing about the River can be rushed. The pace of life on a towboat is mostly slow and deliberate – it takes time to maneuver these behemoths and there is lots of waiting. Going upriver, we are traveling about 3 mph, downriver it might be as "fast" as 6 to 8 mph. Southbound traffic always has the right-of-way, because it takes much longer to stop when going with the current. Since we are northbound, we pull over several times into designated "wait spots" to yield to oncoming barges. Sometimes, weather will slow you down or there may be traffic backed up at a lock – patience is essential.

As we pull up to the lock and dam at Clarksville, Missouri, I am surprised to notice that daylight is already fading. I watch as the Captain angles the tow into position and slowly pushes it into the lock. Five feet is the total clearance between the barges and the walls of the lock and, incredibly, it looks like he has split that distance perfectly into 2 1/2 feet on each side. The deckhands undo the cables and the first nine barges remain in the lock, as The Phyllis pulls back with the remaining six attached. The gates swing shut and the water level inside rises. When it reaches the level of the River above the dam, the gates on that side open, and the barges are pulled out by a winch. The lock is then closed again and the water level lowered; then the towboat and remaining barges enter and the process is repeated. By the time the barges are reattached, the entire "locking through" has taken 90 minutes and it is fully dark.

Again, I stand quietly behind the Captain and watch as we move slowly away from the brightly lighted lock. There is *nothing* beyond the edge of the light. It is as if a black hole is swallowing the barges one foot at a time – my heart clutches as I imagine driving into such blackness. The Captain switches on the massive spotlight mounted above us and sweeps it across the water. Its focused beam slices a narrow swath of light as it passes through the darkness – nothing else can be seen. I was already in awe of the skill required to drive a boat with a protuberance equal to 3 1/3 football fields in daylight; in the dark I find it downright unnerving.

After a hearty dinner with the crew, I walk out onto the back deck. Away from the spotlight and far from any town, in the crisp air of a perfect fall night, the stars take my breath. A moonless sky is allowing an impossible number of them to shine with a brilliance I have rarely seen. I look deeper and deeper, until it seems I am seeing into the far reaches of the universe. Beneath me, the River is so unfathomably black and vast, it seems bottomless and I am on a thin surface suspended amid endless, star-studded space. I feel our planet then as a tiny speck in a boundless cosmos, all of it moving in Divine perfection. I am transfixed, floating, until we pass beneath a bridge and the lights splashing spun gold across the black water bring me back.

Snuggled in bed, I watch the barges appear and disappear with the spotlight. Just as sleep surrounds me like an incoming fog, I sense a change in speed and my eyes pop open. Ahead a drawbridge is breaking in half and swinging aside – I throw on my clothes and race out to photograph it. Twice more I settle in and then fly up and out again when something happens – a tug comes to take one of our barges, or we pull over to let another barge pass. Finally, having accepted that it will be a sleepless night, I lie down fully clothed, ready for whatever comes next. If there is more, however, I miss it, because the hypnotic movement and the rhythmic throbbing of the engine overtake me and I fall into a dreamless sleep as bottomless as the night.

At 4:30, there are voices in the hallway and I smell coffee and bacon. In the galley, Marilyn tells me that, in spite of the hour, I am the last to have breakfast. The sky is a bowl of indigo-black with a sliver of royal blue at the eastern horizon. The deckhands are at work, lifting the hatch covers on every barge and checking inside with a hefty flashlight for any signs of leakage. Then they hoist the ropes, as thick as a man's arm, onto their shoulders and haul them to the opposite side to prepare for the next lock. There is no sense of urgency or rushing, just familiar routines being steadily accomplished.

The morning evaporates and Quincy is just a few hours away. In nearly 24 hours, we will have made 85 River miles. I understand clearly what a rare opportunity I have been given. I've been allowed to experience a slice of this unique life on the River from the inside, without any limitations or attempts to "pretty it up." It's a life of hard work, of constant movement and intimate connection with the fundamental forces of nature. It can be lonely and it can be fulfilling in uncommon ways. While I am sure that some are drawn to it as a job to support their families, it seems to me that something else must develop in order to stick with it. When those who are close to the River speak about it, what I hear is respect for it and an understanding that it must continually change. Often, when they speak about their own lives, they seem to understand the changes there in the same way. It is a valuable lesson that the River offers.

Thank you, Jeff Goldstein, for opening a door to this unseen life on the water, so that I, and many others who have wondered and watched from afar, can sample it. Thanks to the crew of The Phyllis for being so gracious and helpful. Thanks to my dear friend, Ellis Kell, for knocking on that door on my behalf and making something magical happen. Thanks, also, to Serendipity, that force of nature disguised as a little raindrop leading this amazing adventure – you've outdone yourself this time!

PHYLLIS

Chapter Five: The Story Keeper

"Apparently there is
nothing that cannot happen today."

– Mark Twain

Confluences of Brilliance

When Jane Lampton Clemens saw Halley's Comet streak across the sky on a November night in 1835, she knew it to be a good omen for the baby in her womb. Two weeks later, when her son was born prematurely, and many doubted that the five-pound infant would live, Jane was sure that he would not only survive, but would be endowed with special powers. The baby was named Samuel Langhorne Clemens, and he grew to be known the world over as Mark Twain, called by many the "Father of American Literature."

Above me, the sculpted figure of Mark Twain looks out to the silent, immutable Mississippi River as it passes by Hannibal, Missouri. The River shimmers a silvery blue; an hour ago it was a dull slate gray. Twain knew this River as intimately as a lover, in all of its moods. In the days before radar and electronic imaging of land and water, steamboat pilots were required to memorize every serpentine loop, bend and twist in the entire navigable River. In the densest fog or the darkest night, they needed to know at every moment, without thinking, exactly where they were and what was coming next.

The figure above me is a handsome Twain in his mid-20s, who stands confidently behind his pilot's wheel. Everything about his posture and expression seems alert but relaxed, as though he is fully aware of the magnitude of his responsibility and altogether comfortable with it.

Twain claimed that every boy who grew up beside the Mississippi dreamed of becoming a riverboat pilot. When he was granted his pilot's license at the age of 24 and began working the River between St. Louis and New Orleans, he felt he was living the dream for all of them. In *Life on the Mississippi*, Twain says this about those days, "If I have seemed to love my subject, it is no surprising thing...The reason is plain: a pilot, in those days, was the only unfettered and entirely independent human being that lived in the earth."

Just two years later, in 1861, the Civil War erupted, halting all riverboat traffic and signaling the end of the golden era of steamboats. Twain moved away from the Mississippi then, but the Mississippi never left him. For the rest of his days, as he gained great fame as a writer and speaker, acquired and lost vast sums of money, raised a family and traveled the world, the Mississippi River continued to flow in his heart and to saturate his words. Even his assumed name, "Mark Twain," came from a call used by riverboat men to describe water deep enough for a steamboat to pass.

> "Twain knew this River as intimately as a lover, in all of its moods."

The neighborhood that was the backdrop for Mark Twain's boyhood escapades, real and imagined, has been lovingly preserved and restored in Hannibal. His family's home, his father's law office and Becky Thatcher's house are all here, along with a picket fence standing just where the famous whitewashed one stood. The museum is filled with artifacts like original manuscripts and the Norman Rockwell paintings that illustrated the Tom Sawyer and Huck Finn books; even Twain's iconic white suit is here. The spirit of Mark Twain and the characters he created seem to live and breathe here. Still, for me, where I feel Twain most is beside the River, standing on the bank where he must have stood, watching the same River.

In all the photographs I have ever seen of Mark Twain, I have never seen him smile. In fact, he seems to stare through the camera, looking directly at you, brows knitted into an expression that asks, "Who are you and what have you got to say for yourself?" He was friends with the famous and the powerful, but what we love about him is that he was earthy and authentic. We know him as unimpressed by appearances or accumulations, his own or others', and as seeing clearly through any façade to a person's integrity, or dearth of it. He feels accessible, trustworthy and innately brilliant – as genuine and unaffected as the River itself.

Twain looked at life with that same piercing clarity, seeing through the trappings to the truth of it. In 1896, he wrote this in his notebook: "There is in life only one moment and in eternity only one. It is so brief that it is represented by the fleeting of a luminous mote through the thin ray of sunlight – and it is visible but a fraction of a second. The moments that preceded it have been lived, are forgotten and are without value; the moments that have not been lived have no existence and will have no value except in the moment that each shall be lived."

Interestingly, he also knew with a certainty reminiscent of his mother's, when his moments would come to an end. In 1909, he was quoted as saying, "I came in with Halley's Comet in 1835. It is coming again next year, and I expect to go out with it. It will be the greatest disappointment of my life if I don't go out with Halley's Comet. The Almighty has said, no doubt: 'Now here are these two unaccountable freaks; they came in together, they must go out together.'" He was not disappointed. In 1910, Halley's Comet again came near enough to be visible from the earth and made its closest pass on April 20th.

The next day, Mark Twain, age 75, died of a heart attack.

The River is the color of liquid pewter now; a great blue heron stalks the shallows as the day wanes. Through all the comings and goings of herons, comets and humans, the River rolls on, always new and ever the same, always pointing us back to this moment.

A Gypsy, a Giant and a Pot of Gold

I'm convinced that my DNA includes a gene for "gypsy" as certainly as there is one for being tall and having hazel eyes. It has always been there. My first hero was Peter Pan. I remember jumping off my bed *countless* times, certain that if I found just the right happy thoughts, I would be off to Neverland. When the man with the gorgeous black-and-white pony came through the neighborhood and my parents paid for a ride, I calculated snatching the reins from his relaxed hand and galloping down the hill to adventure. My all-time favorite childhood gift was the magical Viewmaster – I walked into those 3D scenes and had tea in tiny wooden cups with strange-looking people in colorful clothing.

The summer I was eight, my beloved grandparents, Nanny and Poppy, set the gypsy free. The day after school was out, we left in a Nash Rambler pulling a pint-sized house trailer and wandered the western U.S. until two days before school started again.

Poppy, when begged, would treat me to a rendition of a gazillion-versed "old road song" from his days traveling and working road construction. Poppy was bigger than life to me and wise in ways I could feel, but not express. He had been on his own since the age of 14 and had lived and worked in many of the places we visited. When he told me a story, I sat motionless and enraptured.

Nanny was my compatriot in every imaginable adventure – she was game for *everything*, so we climbed, waded, and explored while Poppy waited in the shade reading Zane Grey novels. It was heaven. The first time we saw tumbleweed bounding airily across the road, I told them, "If I were a plant, I would be a tumbleweed."

Throughout all the shape-shifting of life since then, there have always been adventures, some extraordinary and some that shine in their simplicity. My daughter, Natalie, and I have a cache of memories from her childhood that shimmer like bubbles, of laughing and singing our way down some highway, belting out any song we could think of, including Christmas carols, while happily ignoring the summer heat. It has never been about the details or the destination, but about travel itself – about surrendering to serendipity with nothing held back.

On this 48th morning of living on the road, I catch my image in the rearview mirror and see the gypsy there. My hair, always curly and a mite willful, borders on wild today and there is high color in my cheeks. The eyes looking back are bright, wide-open

" The Mississippi River stretches herself out in long, luxurious, opalescent curves. "

Day 48 Alton, Illinois

October 10

and seem unusually green. I am reminded of Treasure, the hot-blooded horse I once had (whom I adored and my mother despised, certain that the spirited creature would kill me) and how she would toss her head and flare her nostrils to suck in great gulps of life. Life is being lived full-on and yet easily, without demand.

Everything in God's creation seems brilliantly, vibrantly alive this morning. Two deer spring from nowhere and touch the earth only once as they "boing" across the road ten feet in front of me. A hawk, flashing its ruddy tailfeathers, circles and then dives at incredible velocity into the tall grass, then reappears with a desperately wiggling, but doomed, field mouse in its talons. A misty backwater beckons and, as I tromp through the weeds, a gargantuan black snake fearlessly crosses my path.

Now, for perhaps the first time since leaving home, I shift into a "making good time" mode. I'm headed for Alton, Illinois, and my husband, Mike, is coming to meet me there. I'm grinning as I think of him. If you, too, were born with gypsy in your blood, I wish for you the good fortune of finding a partner like Mike. I can tell you from experience that it will not work if someone tries to tolerate the gypsy in order to have the rest. It can only be that they love the whole package. If you are lucky enough to find *that* relationship – the one in which each of you feels seen and loved, along with your peculiar concoction of traits and quirks, then you have struck gold.

When I see him standing in the hotel parking lot, my heart sings. It takes a massive reorganization of the accumulated detritus that long ago swallowed my passenger's seat to get him in my car, but we manage it and set off, sliding easily into our playful way of being together.

We begin with a visit to the life-sized statue of "the world's tallest man" and one of Alton's most famous native sons, Robert Wadlow. Today, there would be treatment available for his overactive pituitary gland, but, in his lifetime, between 1918 and 1940, there was nothing to stop him from growing to just over 8'11"

tall. We snuggle him up for a photo, measure our shoes against his size 37s and crawl up into his capacious easy chair. He was known as "the gentle giant" and was loved by many, but it must have been a challenging life in a world not made to accommodate him.

Alton is just across the River and 25 miles north of St. Louis, but its personality is a world away from that big, cosmopolitan neighbor. Downtown, it seems there's a party going on. The streets are filled with more big motorcycles than either of us has ever seen in one place. Music wafts down from rooftop patios or rumbles by with the traffic. We find a sunny table at a sidewalk café and kick back to watch the parade of every conceivable variety of bike and biker rolling by. People of all ages seem high-spirited and frisky, relishing what must surely be one of the last weekends of its kind this year.

We plunge into the stream of traffic and head north on the Great Rivers Scenic Byway, which turns out to be one of the most spectacular pieces of the Great River Road that I have seen yet. The winding road perches on a narrow ledge. On one side, it hugs the base of forest-topped white limestone cliffs that shine like alabaster in the sunlight. On the other, the Mississippi River stretches herself out in long, luxurious, opalescent curves. A barge makes its ponderous way upriver and sailboats dance around it like water striders.

This 33-mile scenic byway is bookended by confluences with the Illinois River on the north and the Missouri River on the south. Between them, these two tributaries bring an average of 45 million gallons of water per minute into the Mississippi, so the River does some serious growing up here. The trees along the River Road show mostly green, with only their tips kissed with fall color, but when we ascend the bluffs of Pere Marquette State Park, a white wisp floats in the valley below and the scene is quintessential autumn.

On the southern end of the byway, at the legendary mouth of the Missouri River, we visit the National Great Rivers Museum and the Lewis & Clark Confluence Tower. We tour the Melvin Price Lock & Dam and Mike tries piloting a simulated barge into a lock. After three attempts and three spectacular crashes into the wall, he concedes that it may not be his calling and he has had enough of my uproarious laughter.

We play, laugh, savor some quiet moments and have long meals together and the weekend vanishes. Bittersweet is what I feel as I watch him go. There are 1,100 miles of River left to follow, but knowing that he will be at the end is like knowing there truly is a pot of gold at the end of the rainbow.

Up & Over St. Louis

"Well, which *one*, dammit!?," I snarl at the GPS when it tells me to take the left exit and the traffic demands a quick and irrevocable decision. My nervous system feels like I've been splashed in the face with cold water. For most of the past 50 days on the road, I have dawdled, gawked and paused at will. This, however, is St. Louis, and dawdling could get one run over. Thankfully, the little machine isn't programmed to get in a snit in the face of bad behavior and it continues patiently directing me to my downtown hotel.

It is 4:00 pm when I check in and, although I know the traffic has ramped up another notch, I have a promise to keep. I take a deep breath and set out for a distant suburb to visit a dear friend. It is easier now, I am acclimating to the city, so I arrive without fuss.

She greets me as though she has been perched on the edge of her chair, watching the door. She is Mrs. Lillian Delo Carter, and any words I might use to describe her would fall short of the luminous soul that she is. She cuts off my inquiries about her and demands tales from the road and will brook no skimping on details. She listens as she always has, eagerly receiving every word and asking questions like a seasoned interviewer.

Lil recently moved from our hometown of Springfield to St. Louis to be near her son and to have the support of an assisted living facility. At 92, her incandescent mind is not at all diminished, but her heart is wearing out and her stamina is waning. She seems physically smaller and much more fragile than when I saw her just before I started this journey, and I can see that she is tiring now. She brushes me off impatiently when I mention it; I can see the power of her spirit willing her body to rally. I understand that this conversation is important.

She talks about our special connection, how she has always known that she can tell me anything, how we have fun doing the simplest things and how I am to her like the daughter she lost as a toddler.

She wants to talk about what she calls "our grandest adventure" – the time she accompanied me on a photo shoot in the mountains of Arkansas. With mock indignation, she recounts being rousted out of bed at sunrise to look out the window of our mountaintop lodge. In the valley below, a dazzling white fog was cascading over ridge tops dense with fiery red, orange and yellow trees. It was an unforgettable moment for both of us, and we hold the memory of it now, as delicately as a butterfly.

She is now undeniably tired, but seems satisfied. I promise to stop by again on my way out of town.

I start out on foot in the morning, without plan of course, but wide-open to Serendipity. Just down the block from my hotel is Citygarden, three acres of open spaces, whimsical sculptures, fountains, waterfalls and a mesmerizing silhouette in lights of a couple strolling with the grace of gazelles. The park, surrounded by the density and intensity of the city, is an oasis that invites you to play, wade, touch and slow down.

When I reach the riverfront and the Gateway Arch, I am astounded to find I am completely alone with it. I walk from one massive pedestal to the other, watching the sleekly elegant shape above me transform, as it catches the light differently with every step. I've been here many times, but with no one else in sight, there is something reverent about the experience, like being in a forest of redwoods or a great cathedral.

The Arch is a monument to the courage and pioneering spirit of the men and women who were part of the great westward expansion of our country and also to that same quality in people of every era. For the first time, I can feel that spirit in the boldness and timelessness of this simple, soaring shape.

As I start down the stairs below the Arch, a sightseeing helicopter lifts off in front of me and touches off an internal debate:

- Ooooh, I'd love some aerial shots of the city!
- Forget it – too expensive
- Maybe they would comp it?
- Gayle! This is St. Louis. I'm sure they are deluged with requests from photographers for comped rides. Forget it.

I take another eight steps and hear at *full* volume…

Stop! How do you know if you don't ask?!

So – I spin around, march in, give them a postcard and ask. "Sure," comes the immediate response, "if you want to wait for a couple or a single who want to ride, you can have the extra seat." Barely does my butt touch the chair when a couple arrives and buys the deluxe flight. The bubble-front helicopter has one seat beside the pilot and two in back. When asked where they would like to sit, they glance at my camera gear and each other and say, "Looks like she should be up front." Amazing!

We soar over the River, Busch Stadium and all the downtown landmarks and I never stop shooting. A huge thank you to Gateway Air Tours, to the generous couple I flew with and to Serendipity for not letting me talk myself out of that opportunity!

This morning as I was leaving my hotel, the Hilton Inn at the Ballpark, I left a message for management asking about the possibility of getting onto the roof to shoot the sunset, without having any idea if the roof was even flat or accessible. Now, there is a message saying, "Yes, we can arrange that. Just let us know when you are ready."

A few hours later, armed with fresh batteries, sparkly clean lenses and my sturdiest tripod, I meet

“I’ve been here many times, but with no one else in sight, there is something reverent about the experience, like being in a forest of redwoods or a great cathedral.”

Daniel from Security in the lobby. We take the elevator to the 26th floor, where he unlocks a heavy metal door that opens onto a stairway. Up several flights of stairs, Daniel selects another key from the ring as big around as my arm and unlocks another vault-like door. Fresh air pours in and we step out into *nothing*. The view in every direction is unobstructed and exhilarating, with only a foot-high ridge marking the edge of the building.

The city is washed in warm, late afternoon light and as I shoot, it rapidly shifts to a richly saturated sunset and then to the purplish-blue of twilight. Untold millions of lights wink on and the streets are rivers of gold.

I'm as happy as a kid on Christmas morning, scurrying from one vantage to the next and thrilled with each new scene.

As the sky darkens, Daniel hints gently that work awaits him, so I begin to pack up. Suddenly, enormous floodlights illumine the Arch, so that it shimmers in silver-blue elegance against the gathering night. I glance at Daniel; he smiles, steps back, bows slightly and gestures as an emcee presenting the star attraction. A joyous belly-laugh flies out of me. It is sublime. Thank you to all the wonderful people who play their parts in the magic of this journey and thank you to the Source of all magic.

When I see Lil again, she is more subdued. She cackles delightedly when I tell her the story of my day and her eyes are bright, but her gestures seem heavy and slow. Our farewells are light-hearted, but when I reach the parking lot, I am clutched by the knowledge that I may not see my friend again. I am frozen for a moment, holding a hand to my heart, feeling the grief of losing her.

Then, just as decidedly, I feel her elbow jab my ribs and hear, "Get on with it, girl! There is no time to waste being mopey!" I smile and get back on the road.

Grace

In some places, the stories held by the timeless Mississippi seem nearly buried beneath the chaos and noise of modern life. In others, like Sainte Genevieve, Missouri, tales of the past are kept so vibrantly alive that they seem to call out for us to stop, be still and listen.

Around 260 years ago, the first French Creole settlers arrived in Sainte Genevieve and set about making it home. They planted crops and gardens and built homes in a distinctive vertical log style known as *poteaux-en-terre*. Walls were made from hewn timbers that were set upright in a trench or on a foundation and then mortared with a mix of mud, moss and animal hair.

Those first homes were originally located on the riverbanks, but after a devastating flood in 1785, they were dismantled and moved to higher ground, where some remain today. In fact, Ste. Genevieve, Missouri's oldest town, has the largest collection of French Creole colonial architecture in the country.

Kay Myers, one of my best friends from home, has come to spend the weekend helping me discover Ste. Genevieve. With kudos to Serendipity, today just

"happens" to be Rural Heritage Day, so townsfolk are in period clothing and in a party mood.

Horse drawn wagons shuttle people around the historic district and the air is filled with old-time music and the aroma of apple butter simmering in an iron kettle. You can visit the state's oldest cemetery and make a rubbing from a headstone, if you like. You can learn to juggle, cane a chair or make a rag rug. Ladies are demonstrating lace making, wool spinning and soap making, while men are hitching mules to a plow, blacksmithing and tanning furs.

Kay and I try just about everything, tour most of the historic district, sample most of the available treats, meet some interesting people, catch up on girlfriend talk and finally laugh ourselves to sleep.

Our time together flies and, before I know it, I am standing in the hotel parking lot waving goodbye to her. Then it hits me. Without warning, I am blindsided by a freight train of homesickness. Knowing that my

friend will be back in our hometown by lunchtime, and that I will not see it again until Thanksgiving, fills me with cold aloneness. I had expected that there might be times like this – it is, after all, a long journey. Still, the surprise and the intensity of it fairly knocks the wind out of me and I stand in the murky pre-dawn, wondering what to do next.

Take it to the River, of course.

The cold, damp air is bone-chilling and the inky sky shows just a thin streak of orange in the east. The riverbank is littered with trash – I tromp over it, kick at it and plunk down on a fallen tree. The River is dark purple and, as I stare into its moving depths, it stirs a familiar response in me.

I know that the River is simply being the River, but in its presence, I feel unconditional love that is blind to my current emotional state. Thus ignored, its power is negated. It is just sadness, after all – it requires no fixing or resisting. It is as valid as joy – just let it flow. I close my eyes and meditate until I am warmed by the sunrise.

When I look, the current is etching deep blue shadows in an orange River and the emerging sun unrolls a path of golden light straight to my heart. I am unclenched. I breathe it in and feel it warm and enliven everything. I smile, stretch, walk to the car and start driving, with no intention.

I drive out onto the high, narrow levee. To my left, the River is veiled from view by a marshy forest; to my right, a

“ The leaders circle back and make another pass over the flock, this time lifting up followers in their wake. ”

broad, flat valley is bisected by a shallow backwater slough. I can see fluttery white movement on the narrow strip of water. As I get closer, I can see through my telephoto lens that the surface is covered with the ample bodies of thousands of American White Pelicans.

As I watch, there is a stirring and a dozen birds on the near end of the massive flock take to the air. They make a low pass over the others, rousing them to unfold and flap their black-edged wings. The leaders circle back and make another pass over the flock, this time lifting up followers in their wake. Then, a churning storm cloud of white and black fills the air and even from this distance I can hear the clamor of their calls.

They whirl and circle each other, as if gathering momentum and determining direction. Then, as one mind, they create jagged V's and glide toward the River behind me, many passing directly over me. They are so close that I can see their thick, fourteen-inch beaks piercing the air and their stocky, gleaming white bodies held aloft by magnificent ten-foot wingspans. I watch, breathless, as they disappear behind the trees.

What happens next seems unbelievable. I don't see it coming, but as the last of the pelicans drop out of sight, I hear movement in the air above me. Incredibly, there is an immense Bald Eagle doing some sort of aerial acrobatics. It spins and tumbles through the air, then folds in its wings and hurtles downward. Then, it spreads its wings, splays its talons and soars upward. A few more twisting somersaults and then it climbs high and seems to rest on the air.

Then, in a dramatic finish that stops my heart, it makes a wide arc with wings fully outstretched, swoops low and passes directly over me before rocketing out over the valley. I have no explanation and I have never experienced anything like this.

I lean against my car, stunned, depleted and tearful with gratitude. Less than two hours ago, I stumbled to the River, tangled in emotions. Now, I have not just been untangled, but dazzled and finally dissolved into the unspeakable beauty and majesty of nature.

Lead on, little raindrop – I am yours!

Better Than Spinach

In spite of the frosty air, I'm cruising with the windows open and the heater blasting, hoping to improve the air in this funky-smelling car. There must be a rotting apple core lurking somewhere, intermingling its scent with that of the bulging bag of dirty laundry. The floor beneath my mud-caked boots is crunchy with grit and even the gas and brake pedals are coated in river mud.

The plastic file box that rides shotgun, with files color-coded by state, is lost in an avalanche of maps, brochures and notes that haven't quite gotten filed yet. I am days behind in posting on the blog, answering emails and backing up photos, and I am hungry for a dose of quiet riverbank time. My vehicle and I are both a bit road weary.

As I arrive in Chester, Illinois, I am greeted by a bronze statue of Popeye, the beloved spinach-guzzling sailor, who was born in the mind of Elzie Segar, who was himself born here in 1894. As I stand looking up at the pipe-smoking, bulbous-cheeked, crusty old sailor, he seems to be saying, "Aaww, all yer needs is a big can o' me spinach!" While I hope there's another way (the stringy, lifeless stuff in cans seems to me barely related to actual spinach), there is no doubt I could use the

"If I were granted the privilege of watching the sun rise and set over this River 10,000 times, I know that no two would be alike."

Day 55 Chester, Illinois *October 17*

kind of muscle-ballooning, super-rejuvenating power surge that he got from downing the stuff.

As usual, Serendipity is one step ahead of me. Sandra Starr, innkeeper at The Stone House B&B, has invited me to stay with her these next two days. The house, which was originally built in 1846 as a church, sits atop a bluff with a grand view of the Mississippi.

Sandra, a gypsy herself, has filled her home with warm colors and treasures from her travels. When I see my second story room and the view from the private balcony, I feel better already. When she tells me I am her only guest and invites me to set up my office at the dining table or on the broad front porch, to do my laundry, fix my soup in her kitchen and just be at home, my response is a long, deep, "Aaahhh."

Although I give myself permission to sleep in and miss the sunrise, the River apparently vetoes that notion. I'm nudged out of bed before first light, and, as I stand beside the 1942 Chester Bridge, watching the lacy reflection of its iron trusses on the surface below, I know that she was right.

A follower of my blog recently wrote to tell me her memories of "going uptown with Grandpa to get the mail" in a small Mississippi River town. All the old gents passing time there greeted each other, not with a comment about the weather, but about the River. They might say, "She's ridin' mighty high this mornin'," or "The Mississippi is always a woman, but she ain't no lady today," or, the one I'm sure they would use this morning, "She's lookin' smooth as a baby's bottom."

If I were granted the privilege of watching the sun rise and set over this River 10,000 times, I know that no two would be alike – this one is gentle, sweet, creamy pink and a balm to my system. I drive out on the levee and find that everything is kissed with a barely perceptible sheen of frost, diffusing edges and blending it all into a pearlescent watercolor stretching away to the horizon. I park, close my eyes and drift in a meditation that enfolds me like a cloud. Then, it's time to get to work.

Now, less than 48 hours after arriving, my rolling house is in order. I am caught up, tidied up, rested up and pumped up! I honk and wave at Popeye as I leave town and call out, "Shiver me timbers, Matey – just look at me now! And, I didn't even have to eat canned spinach!"

Braided Tales

Little Erica Cooley takes the biggest breath she can manage and successfully blows out the big "2" candle on her blue-and-orange birthday cake, bringing a wave of applause from her adoring family. She tugs off the party hat, crosses her arms and waits serenely as her mom cuts the cake. Then, already knowing that the camera loves her, she turns her porcelain-doll face toward me with a wide-open look of innocence that could melt stone.

Erica's grandparents, Tom and Terri Neumeyer, welcomed me an hour ago to their B&B in Cape Girardeau, Missouri, and promptly invited me to join in this family celebration. After the party, Tom marks a map with local sites and favorite vantage points, one of which is this quiet park with a peninsula that provides perfect alignment to the sleek Bill Emerson Memorial Bridge.

With my tripod and camera set up on the riverbank and my apple, crackers and peanut butter dinner beside me, I await the magic of twilight. A young couple who had been sitting with their arms entangled and their heads together disengage and walk toward their car. A boy and his grandpa who had been fishing pack up to head home. Now, it is the River and me.

As the light falls, the scent of the River rises – familiar, but ever unknowable, rich with life and with something untamable. When I put my attention on the sound of the River, it whispers wordless wisdom with a barely audible rippling.

The bridge lights switch on and I am launched into action. Two gleaming silver triangles hover above the water, which is perfectly mirroring the deep cobalt of the sky. Long, quivering stripes of liquid silver and gold spill toward me.

In fifty-seven days of accompanying this majestic River, she has yet to repeat a color or mood. I fall more in love with her every day.

Some call Cape Girardeau "the place where the River turns a thousand tales." Stories are cherished here as history, as entertainment and as art. After several floods inundated the historic downtown, a concrete floodwall was erected, but townsfolk found it unsightly. The answer was to create the Mississippi

River Tales Mural – 24 painted panels that stretch for 1,100 feet and chronicle life beside the River from prehistory to the present. Cape Girardeau also hosts an annual Storytelling Festival, and hundreds will come to hear nationally-acclaimed yarn-spinners captivate their audiences.

Some stories, though, are hard to hear. A beautiful park just north of town memorializes the horrific suffering and cruelty endured by 16,000 Cherokee people, as they trudged past, on what is now known as the Trail of Tears. After President Andrew Jackson signed the Indian Removal Act in 1830, all Indians living east of the Mississippi were removed from their homelands and forced to walk to Indian Territory, in what is now western Oklahoma.

"The beauty of this place is as heartbreaking as its memories."

At the Trail of Tears State Park Visitors Center, I read the words of a woman who made the walk as a small child. Without warning and without time to gather their belongings, she says, soldiers drove the family out of their home. They were held in a stockade with hundreds of other families until the 1,000-mile forced march ensued. In the grueling year-long ordeal that followed, as many as 4,000 Cherokee people died of malnutrition, exposure and diseases.

I return to the Trail of Tears State Park to catch the sunrise from the scenic overlook. Below me is the riverbank where cooking fires would have smoldered that winter of 1838 and 1839 while Cherokee people waited, sometimes weeks or months, to be ferried across the Mississippi.

All is serene and lovely now. Sky and River are painted baby blue with strokes of delicate pink presaging the rising sun. As the morning comes into its glory, tiny clouds as luminous as angel wings dot the sky. Behind and above me, amber and red leaves catch the light and glow like embers. The beauty of this place is as heartbreaking as its memories.

There is a plaiting of story lines in my mind then. The Trail of Tears march, I realize, occurred during the glory days of steamboating on the Mississippi, when there were at least 1,200 paddlewheelers regularly churning up and down the River. Undoubtedly, steamboats would have passed the Cherokee encampments. Few Cherokee people had ever seen such a thing. What was that like? What was it like for the travelers, peering down from the decks, leaning on the gingerbread railing? Did they understand what was happening to the people on the bank?

There are no separate stories. Like the thousands of tiny streams that come together to form the Mississippi, all the stories of this journey are ultimately intertwined, and the River is the great story keeper.

What Remains

It takes a moment of standing dumbly in front of the gas pump before I realize that there *is* no credit card slot because this is not pay-at-the-pump, nor is it even pay-before-you-pump. There is simply an old guy leaning on the counter inside, watching.

"Howdy," he says flatly and ambles to the tiny TV shouting from the corner and turns down the sound. He looks at me as if measuring his next thought, then says, "Fine mornin' innit." Newspapers splay across the floor beside a worn leather armchair placed where he can rest his feet on the window ledge, next to an overflowing ashtray.

The morning sun shines lamely through the dirty window and exaggerates the haze of stale, smoke-filled air. There's a cooler of drinks, a rotating rack of chips, cartons of cigarettes stacked behind him, a few shelves of gum and candy and a fishbowl of peppermints on the counter. All remaining surfaces are covered with a mishmash of stuff that has the look of having rested there a long time.

After another appraising glance, he ventures further, "Where ya headed today?" In that instant, I understand that he doesn't *want* to modernize those pumps because he likes the company in his little den. When I answer that I'm not really sure, he cocks his head, bumps the bill of his ball cap with his fist and looks concerned. "Need some directions?" he asks, trying hard to get a read on me.

So, I explain. His head snaps back in surprise, "Well, I'll be! Ain't that somethin'! That's a long ride, young lady. All by yourself?" Although he clearly doubts the wisdom of such a thing, he immediately wants to help by orienting me to where I am and where I'm headed.

He tells me that I have reached the end of the Midwest. "Once you come down off'n the hill south o' Cape," he says, "you're in the Miss'sippi Delta and you won't see 'nother hill on this side o' the River clean to the Gulf." He has some stern warnings then about some rough areas ahead and he follows me out the door, wagging his finger and twice repeating a dead-serious, "You be *careful* now, ya hear?"

I cross the River to mark the remaining miles of the very long state of Illinois. For nearly 600 miles, the River has sculpted the state's western boundary and the differences in geography, climate and culture from the northern border with Wisconsin to the southern end where it meets Kentucky, are tremendous.

The southernmost tip of the state is a tapered peninsula, shaped by the Mississippi and the Ohio Rivers coursing toward one another. The Ohio, itself a river of consequence, has gathered so much water over its 981-mile course, that its addition more than doubles the flow of the Mississippi. On river navigation maps, this confluence marks the transition from the Upper to the Lower Mississippi River and I am reminded that only 953 miles remain before the River ceases to exist.

The last town on the narrowing spit of land between the rivers is Cairo (pronounced *KAY-ro*). Although I have come through this region many times, I have never before passed beneath the iron archway proclaiming, "Historic Downtown Cairo," and entered the town. The first few blocks look tired and decrepit, but as I reach the heart of town, it is much worse than that. In fact, the eerie scene that stretches for block after block looks like a movie set for a disaster film.

Day 58 Cairo, Illinois October 20

Decay and devastation line both sides of the street; some structures appear burned, some look as if they were bombed and some have simply succumbed to neglect and collapsed into heaps of bricks, timbers and rubble. Doorways are boarded up or left gaping open to expose mounds of trash and debris. Brick arches frame holes where even the plywood that replaced windows is rotting and falling away. A wooden awning, which once sheltered customers entering a business, was long ago left to deteriorate where it fell across the sidewalk.

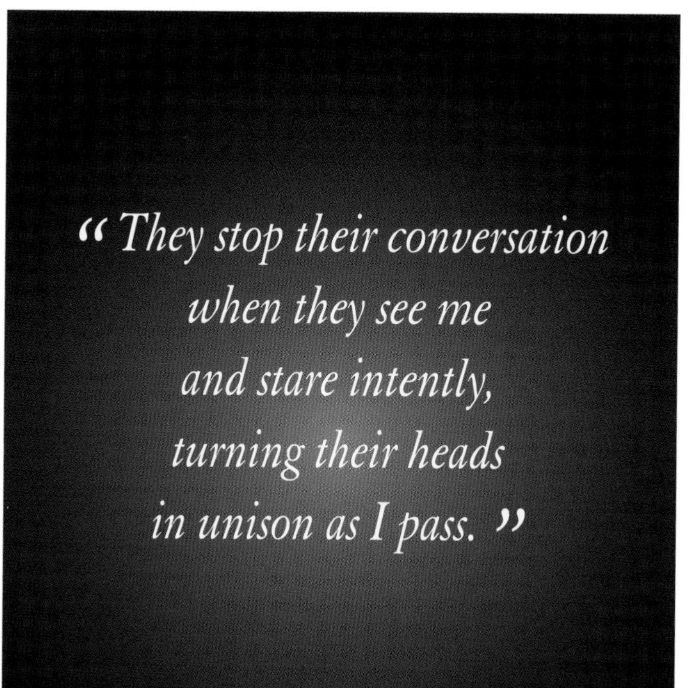

There are no signs of life, just the slow crumbling and decomposing of what was once clearly a thriving town. Here and there, Kudzu vines seem to be attempting to grow a blanket for the enormous carcass, but it's a daunting task.

Although it is 10:30 on a sunny Tuesday morning, there is no one on the street except one small group of young African American men. They stop their conversation when they see me and stare intently, turning their heads in unison as I pass. Mine is the only vehicle on the street.

As a photographer, I know that dozens of darkly compelling images lurk amid these ruins and I briefly consider stopping, but I do not. There is the memory of my finger-wagging, chain-smoking, gas station buddy warning me to "stay clear of Cairo." There is a chilling, sinister atmosphere to the whole place and there is some other vague reticence. Although I seldom feel fearful or unsafe, as a woman traveling alone, I respect and heed my instincts. When my internal warning system says, "Don't go there," I obey without question.

So, what on earth happened here? At my first opportunity, I begin to ask and the story that emerges entwines hatred, racial conflict, organized crime, corruption, violence and fear into a noose that choked the life from Cairo.

Local historians tell me that racial discord has plagued Cairo since before the Civil War, when some citizens secretly made the town an important stop on the Underground Railroad, while others vehemently supported slavery. During the war, allegiances in this area were mixed and, although Union troops were stationed at this strategically important River port, there were also violent gangs of renegade Confederate supporters that terrorized the countryside.

When the war ended, Cairo became a staging area for black refugees from the South. Although most of the former slaves moved on to find work or returned to the South to become sharecroppers, several thousand stayed in Cairo, dramatically changing the racial composition and exacerbating racial animosity.

The deeper one looks into Cairo's troubled history, the darker is the story that emerges. Even as business owners prospered, and the town's population grew to an all-time high of 15,000 by 1920, there are accounts of racially-motivated violence and gruesome lynchings by jeering, angry mobs. When river and railroad traffic declined and the Great Depression began, the town's economy spiraled downward and the population dwindled.

By the 1950s, organized crime moved into Cairo and established profitable enterprises in illegal bootlegging and gambling. Their success drew the attention of rival mobs, who attempted to take over. The ensuing turf wars between gangsters brought more bloodshed, and more of Cairo's citizens fled.

In the 1960s, when racial violence was erupting around the country, the toxic brew of hatred and mistrust in Cairo had been simmering for so long, that it reached a boiling point very quickly. Murders, retaliations, protests and riots raged, and businesses were burned and destroyed. In the summer of 1967, local law enforcement was so overwhelmed by the rampage that the National Guard was called in to restore order.

The mayhem, however, continued for years, as the white community created a "citizen's protection group" known as the "White Hats" and the black community formed a coalition called the "Cairo United Front." In 1969, the Cairo United Front launched a boycott of white-owned businesses, which was essentially every business in town, and, by 1971, nearly all had shut down and been abandoned. Cairo had been strangled to death by malice.

Today, there are only about 2,800 people living in Cairo. They live with bleak hopes in a blighted town that cannot afford basic services, with a high crime rate and an extreme level of poverty.

I realize now what the "something else" was that stopped me from photographing Cairo. It's a question of propriety, or ethics, that I have faced before in my career. Where is the line that, when crossed, has one walking in exploitation? The icy stares of the young men on the street told me how it would feel to watch a stranger, who could afford to travel, *take* photographs and drive off, picking the bones of the carcass and leaving nothing in return.

Cairo's sad story seems to want to be told, but with more respect than that.

Chapter Six: A Gumbo of Cultures

“Every day, I see the amazing diversity of Americans in the way we speak, what we eat and how we spend our time – and right in the center of appreciating those differences, I am shown what is universal and connects us all.”

– Gayle Harper

Dichotomies and Mysteries

I had imagined that the trees edging the checkerboard fields of corn, soybeans and wheat in southeast Missouri would be glowing with autumn colors. Instead, the branches are hung with lifeless clumps of shriveled brown leaves. The late morning sun is diffused behind a hazy veil of dense, dusty air. When I stop for coffee, bleary-eyed farmers tell me it was June the last time they had a good rain in these parts.

In the fields, massive moving clouds of dust engulf and dwarf the barely-visible combines creating them. I imagine the sleep-deprived farmer sealed inside the cab, hypnotized by the motion and the perfection of the rows, reaching again for his coffee thermos. It is harvest time

Day 59 Charleston, Missouri *October 21*

and all else must wait until the crops are in.

In a curious juxtaposition, the River is straining at its banks as it rushes by this parched, thirsty land. Remember the weeks of rain up north that seemed interminable? The great swollen bulge of all that water is now making its way downriver, sliding southward like a python's meal. Although that seems a strange anomaly to me, folks here in Mississippi County, Missouri, are accustomed to nature's vagaries. Some of us watch the weather to decide on a jacket or umbrella, but life in this farming culture is governed by and synchronized with the continual flux of weather and seasons.

I have been here before – at a time when everything in the natural world seemed altogether opposite of this. Trees and grass in a thousand shades of fresh, vibrant green surrounded dark, moist fields being planted or already dotted with tiny sprouts.

In the town of Charleston, where I and 35,000 other folks had come for the annual Dogwood-Azalea Festival, the extravagance of spring blooms was breathtaking. Since 1952, the Molly French Garden Club has been distributing species of dogwood trees and azalea bushes, selected to suit the local climate, to Charleston's citizens. As a result, this charming town of 5,000 is transformed each April into a fairyland of lacy white, soft pink and deep fuchsia blooms.

Dogwood trees, dense with delicate white flowers, reach toward each other from both sides of the street, and the sidewalks along the six-mile Dogwood Azalea Trail are filled with a parade of admirers. Gracious, but comfortable, old homes have wide front porches with wicker furniture and swings and hanging baskets of flowers or ferns. Everywhere, lovingly tended beds of blooming plants and shrubs are at their peak of perfection.

The four-day Dogwood-Azalea Festival, which began in 1968, has all the prerequisites of a great small town party – there's the parade, carnival, fish fry, ice cream social and live music, but the centerpiece of it all is the Candlelight Tour. At twilight on Saturday night, the magic is switched on as townsfolk set out 6,000 candle-and-paper-bag luminaries to line the sidewalks. Spotlights, buried beneath and within the flowering trees and shrubs, transform them into glowing wonders.

Porch lights shine as neighbors gather and call out to each other to come by for a mint julep or sweet tea. More than once, I am invited to join a gathering and tempted with chocolate-covered strawberries, spicy cashews and homemade ice cream. Herds of kids with popsicles dripping down their arms roam freely, their laughter as sweet as the flower-scented air. Visitors stop to chat and snap photos and every face is warmed by the candlelight and softened by the enchantment of it all.

As I bask in the memories of that weekend, one stands out as iconic of my Charleston experience. Early Sunday morning, I was kneeling in someone's front yard, composing a scene framed by a tire swing, when I was startled from my concentration by a jolly, "Good morning!" I looked up to see a boy of about thirteen on his bicycle, waving exuberantly and beaming a smile. I smiled and waved back and he grinned as he pedaled on down the street, tossing newspapers from the pouch strapped across his chest. It felt like we were two characters in a Norman Rockwell painting.

Now, another juxtaposition arises. In my mind, that boy's open, happy face bumps up against the faces of the young men on the street in Cairo, Illinois. Their dark, glowering stares spoke of life experiences so far removed from the newspaper boy's, that it is incomprehensible that these two towns are separated only by the River and sixteen miles of road. Every town, it seems, like every human, follows its own unique path.

I came to Charleston that first time knowing no one, but now, I am welcomed back by good friends that I made then. For two days, I am buoyed by laughter, lively conversation and fine home cooking, in the company of Claudia and Randy Arington and Silvey and Sam Barker.

On my last evening, Silvey wants to take me to a place she loves – the Towosahgy State Historic Site near her farm in East Prairie, Missouri. Chris Crabtree, a naturalist and historian at the site, and a friend of Silvey's, meets us there and, together, we walk to the top of Temple Mound.

Chris explains that Temple Mound is the largest and tallest of the seven earthen mounds at this site that were built by people of the Mississippian Culture, between 800 and 1500 A.D. Temple Mound, where the chief and his family lived, and ceremonies were held, was once surrounded by a fortified village containing 300 or more dwellings.

Chris, whose chiseled features and dark eyes are evidence of his own Native American heritage, uncovers a small pottery shard, half-hidden in the grass. As he turns it over in his hand and then puts it in mine, and says that it is probably over 1,000 years old, the quiet reverence in his manner touches me.

An almost-full moon rises in the east, as the sun slips away in the west. Chris says goodbye, but invites

“I cannot say if the rhythmic jangling sound I hear might be coming from some distant farm, from some unfamiliar insect or from the ankle bells of ancient dancers.”

us to stay as long as we like. After a moment, Silvey says quietly, “I’m going to walk back to the car now. I think you should have some time here alone.” I am surprised by that, but appreciative, and I sit down on the broad, flat mound top in the gathering dusk.

I am aware of a deep stillness beneath the gentle evening sounds of crickets and birds. My spine feels anchored into the earth, which feels alive and welcoming. There is an unmistakable energy of *presence*.

I cannot say if the rhythmic jangling sound I hear might be coming from some distant farm, from some unfamiliar insect or from the ankle bells of ancient dancers. Nor can I explain the wall of sharply cold air that I walk into and out of again, as I descend the mound.

I can only say that I am thankful that this prehistoric site is now protected and preserved, honoring those who lived here and allowing the rest of us to experience it, each in our own way. Not everything needs to be figured out.

What If...

The River's path here looks like mine often does – it makes a U-turn and heads back north, then makes a big, counter-clockwise circle and nearly meets itself coming and going, before getting back to the business of moving all this water southward.

The soil cradling the Lower Mississippi is much softer than the often rocky bed of the Upper River and is much more amenable to such wanderings. It is not difficult to imagine that one day the River might take a shortcut across the few miles of low, swampy land at the neck of the oxbow, and leave New Madrid looking at a curved lake instead of a River. For now, though, this drowsy little town of 3,200 souls sits at the very top of the loop, where eight miles of River can be seen curving up from the left and away to the right.

For most of us, what we know about New Madrid has to do with earthquakes – in one tense or another – either the one that happened, the one that might happen or the one that didn't. The one that happened was mighty. In fact, it was the most powerful earthquake *ever* in the 48 contiguous states. There were no seismographs around in the winter of 1811 and 1812, but, by using other evidence, scientists have determined that each of the three quakes that struck during a span of three months was at least a magnitude of 7.5 on the Richter scale.

When violent shaking threw folks from their beds at 2:15 a.m. on December 16th, they ran into the street and clung to each other in terror. Trees crashed to the ground around them and their homes waved, buckled and collapsed into heaps. There was a deafening roar as the earth rolled in waves and split open into vast crevasses. Light flashed upward from the ground in a terrifying display, that we now know is the result of quartz crystals being compressed underground, but to the frightened settlers seemed like hell arising.

Great geysers erupted and the air was dense with foul-smelling smog. Birds screeched and animals bellowed and ran in wild, blind panic. On the River, massive sections of bank collapsed and great sections of the river bed were shoved upward, causing huge upstream waves, swamping boats and prompting many reports of the River running backward for a time. Understandably, many were certain that it was the end of the world.

Earthquakes are different in the middle of the continent than on the west coast – they have a much greater reach. The series of quakes in 1811-1812 brought down cabins and chimneys as far away as Cincinnati and St. Louis, and people felt it from the Rocky Mountains to New York City and from Montreal to Cuba. Casualties were low, however, because the region was so sparsely populated at that time. New Madrid, in fact, with its 400 citizens, was the largest settlement on the Mississippi between St. Louis and Natchez, Mississippi, a distance of nearly 600 miles. It is a very different situation today.

" Understandably, many were certain that it was the end of the world. "

Seismic activity is recorded almost daily along the New Madrid fault. People in the area are accustomed to feeling tremors and there have been many small

Reprinted with the permission of the New Madrid Historical Museum.

earthquakes. While some experts say it is unlikely that there will be another event as powerful as the one 200 years ago, most seem to agree that a lesser earthquake, possibly a magnitude 6, could happen at any time and may, in fact, be "overdue."

Given the major population centers and the complex infrastructure that now exist, the effects of that would be catastrophic. It is believed that damage would be spread over 15 to 20 states and that there would likely be thousands of casualties. Millions of people would be in need of shelter and medical care, and damaged bridges and roads would hinder disaster relief. Fires would rage uncontrolled as water supplies and electricity would be disrupted. Undeniably, it's awful to imagine.

That brings us to the crazy story of the earthquake that didn't happen. Science has evolved in astounding ways in the past two centuries, but it remains nearly impossible to predict an earthquake. Iben Browning believed otherwise.

Browning was a native Texan, living in New Mexico, who had degrees in philosophy, zoology, genetics and bacteriology (but nothing related to earth science or seismology). He had an interest in weather and climatology, and he devised a theory that a particular alignment of the earth, moon and sun would create tidal forces capable of causing a major earthquake.

Based on that, he predicted that there was a 50/50 chance of a major quake occurring along the New Madrid fault on or near December 3rd, 1990. (Now… it seems to me that 50/50 is about the same chance as every other day, but no matter…) The story was picked up by a handful of news outlets, and a fire-storm of alarm was ignited.

Scary headlines appeared, which generated more headlines, and the snowballing story began showing up in national and international media. Earthquake experts continually rejected the prediction, as being completely without merit and having no basis in science, but those voices were largely ignored. Sales of earthquake insurance soared and, soon, stores were selling out of bottled water, batteries and canned food.

The National Guard announced that they would conduct an earthquake drill at that time and set up a mobile hospital nearby, but maintained that it was

"for practice" and not related to the prediction. Local schools decided to close for two days, because "what if" it happened and they had been warned, but hadn't listened. Many local residents made plans to be out of town, while others decided to sleep outside in tents (remember – it was December!). Some others, however, saw rare opportunities inherent in all this fuss.

Media people were coming to town – lots of them. The New Madrid Chamber of Commerce designed and printed souvenir t-shirts and shot glasses. The local bar and grill added a new menu item, the "Quakeburger," served with a jagged split across the top bun. By December 1st, the streets of downtown New Madrid were clogged with satellite trucks and news vehicles, and every motel in the region was overflowing. Reporters, desperate for stories to file, interviewed locals until many grew so weary of answering the same questions, they went into hiding. No one had ever seen anything like this.

December 3rd dawned and the earth stood still. The 300 news personnel roaming the streets were reduced to interviewing one another and filing non-news stories with bits like, "Well, so far the levee is still holding firm." They watched their drinking glasses and waited for something to wiggle. No seismic activity at all was recorded during those days – not even a tremor. The media circus packed up and left, leaving the citizens of New Madrid shaking their heads in amazement.

Virginia Carlson was the Director of the New Madrid Historical Museum in 1990, as she is today. She chuckles as she recalls that unforgettable time and waves her hand at the new section of the Museum. "All this," she says smiling, "was built with money we made selling souvenirs during the Great Media Quake of 1990. It was a terrific windfall for New Madrid. Actually," she continues, "it did raise public awareness about the possibility of earthquakes and we are now better prepared because of it." Everything serves a purpose, it seems.

Folks in New Madrid are pragmatic about the threat of an earthquake, just as people on the southeast coast are about hurricanes and in the Midwest about tornadoes. The one thing certain about life is that it will always remain unpredictable.

I'm on the road again and the world has that luminous, rosy sheen that happens for only a few minutes just before sunrise. A foolhardy squirrel that was safely across the road turns back in a heartbeat and darts in front of my wheel. It is too late to react. I cringe and wait. Then, miraculously, I see him in my rearview mirror, bounding into the grass, a fraction of a second having made all the difference.

There just might be an earthquake today or a truck in my lane around the next bend, so I put down the window and take in all the cool, crisp air my lungs can handle and feel thankful for being alive in this moment.

Frog Legs and Eggs? Oh, My!

I stand quietly at the railing, watching ghostly swirls of mist rise from the surface and then melt into a gauzy, hovering layer.

Only a handful of car ferries still operate across the Mississippi and the slow, intimate experience of being *on* the River trumps so magnificently that of zooming across on an interstate bridge, that it was a no-brainer. Like a kid, I watch the receding and approaching shorelines to guess the halfway point and mark the state line between Missouri and Kentucky. Too quickly, I am delivered to the opposite shore, and I take the first road heading south.

It's the first run of the morning for the Dorena-Hickman ferry. Without any pretense at having made a decision to do so, I have backtracked in order to ride it a second time. The first, while visiting my friends in Charleston, Missouri, disappeared in a frenzy of shooting photos and asking questions. This morning,

The land is low, flat and sparsely populated and feels somehow desolate. If there is a state line marker, I miss it, but a change in the surface of the road and the shape of the highway signs, tells me that I have crossed into Tennessee. There have been no towns and I've had coffee and breakfast on my mind for some time, when

Day 62 Tiptonville, Tennessee *October 24*

“Nature is perfect – problems arise when we mess with it.”

a solitary café surrounded by a ring of pickups appears. I slide in among the trucks with gun racks in the windows and flat-bottomed boats behind.

A wall of dense cigarette smoke mingled with old grease stops me just inside the door. I pause, considering coffee to go. Then I realize that, one by one, every conversation in the room has stopped and all heads have turned toward me. A room full of men in head-to-toe camo is staring at me as if I have two heads, and I have just trampled on sacred ground. We all freeze – with me taking stock of the situation, and them continuing to stare in silence.

Confused, but not wanting to appear intimidated, I stand tall, look a couple of them in the eye, nod, smile and do an about-face. Out front, I actually check to see if I missed a sign with something like, “Members Only Men’s Club,” but find no such warning. As a traveler, I’ve grown quite used to having patrons of local cafés notice that someone “not from here” has come in, but I hardly know what to make of this experience.

Down the road, in an area of fishing resorts and family restaurants, I try again. The waitress says something that lands in my ear like one long, twangy compound word. When I ask her to repeat it, it sounds the same, so I smile and nod. I must have said yes to coffee because a steaming mug of very stout, very black brew shows up with the menu.

The breakfast specials include “Frog Legs and Eggs,” “Quail and Eggs” and “Bologna and Eggs.” Happily, although it’s not on the menu, the cook agrees to a veggie omelet, which arrives, curiously, with a bowl of white gravy. Clearly, Toto, we have plunked down into a strange new land!

In between reading about “Slingshot Charlie Taylor,” a legendary local who was so skilled with a slingshot that he could hit ducks, snuff cans and pennies in midair, I eavesdrop a little. (Well, it can’t really be helped when eating alone and, besides, I rationalize, it’s helping me acclimate to this new culture.)

In the booth behind me, a girl of about nine with her Grandpa is counting the days that remain of her visit with him and Grandma. When she comes up with five, she says, “OK, what if we go fishing three days and hunting two days?” Grandpa, who sounds like a “gruff outside and teddy bear inside” kind of guy, agrees with mock grumbling. When I can be a little discreet, I look around to see Grandpa, in a battered and stained fishing hat, smile at the adorable, freckled girl with a pony tail poking out the back of her ball cap. He is obviously putty in her hands.

I am in Lake County, Tennessee, where most of life revolves around the fishing and hunting made possible by Reelfoot Lake and its surrounding wetlands. Originally an ancient oxbow of the “Old Mississippi,” the lake was reshaped when the land heaved upward and then collapsed during the New Madrid earthquakes of 1811-12. The depression thus created in the earth soon filled with water and submerged a vast, swampy forest.

Two hundred years later, since many of the drowned trees are rot-resistant cypress, they still stand in the lake, peppering the surface with their tops. Many more, however, lurk just below, as unwary boaters frequently discover. The best way to negotiate these waters is slowly, in a flat-bottomed “jon boat” and to know what you are doing.

The shallow 18,000-acre lake is rimmed with magnificent bald cypress trees, some that are 500 years old. They poke their sculpted, knobby knees above the surface along the shadowy shoreline, creating eerie, primordial scenes. I’m told to watch my feet, as “It’s real

snaky territory," and I do see one skimming atop the water and another slithering into the grass. Frogs and turtles plop into the water as I come near and birds squawk a warning. It is teeming with life – small wonder it is a Mecca for outdoor enthusiasts.

As I begin to meet people, I learn that there is a long history of contention over these rich natural resources. In the early 1900s, a group of wealthy investors bought much of the shoreline and subsequently claimed to own the fishing rights on the lake as well. Folks in this wild and essentially lawless region depended on the lake for sustenance, so they quickly took matters in their own hands.

A vigilante group called the "Night Riders" was formed and there are dark tales of hangings, shootings, brutal retaliations and narrow escapes into the swamp. The violence escalated until the state militia was eventually called in to put an end to it. A century later, the Night Riders are long gone and the lake is safely in the public domain, but strong differences remain and the issues are complex.

A downriver friend has insisted that I meet her friend, Jim Johnson, while I am here, so I call and we meet for coffee. Jim's easy-going manner, his Tennessee drawl and low, slightly raspy voice draw me in like an old blues singer, as he tells me about his life.

Jim grew up, like his father and grandfather, fishing, hunting, trapping and guiding in the small Reelfoot Lake community of Walnut Log. The one hundred or so residents needed only the lake for their sustenance and their lives moved in harmony with the rhythms of nature.

As a young man, Jim left home for college, became a biologist and, after a few years of working in Washington, D.C., for the National Wildlife Federation, came home to Tennessee to work with the Tennessee Wildlife Resources Agency. He soon found that Reelfoot was no longer the healthy, abundant lake of his boyhood, and he knew that it was up to him to understand what was happening and to do what he could to help. As it turns out, that put him smack in the center of a cauldron of controversy.

I am curious to understand myself, at least as much as a non-scientific passerby can grasp in a short time, and Jim, with his blend of natural wisdom and scientific knowledge, is the perfect teacher. "It is essentially the same answer," he tells me, "that we hear for every environmental problem on earth. Nature is perfect; problems arise when we mess with it."

Reelfoot Lake is the child, Jim explains, created by and naturally nurtured by the parent, the Mississippi River. Before human intervention in the form of levees and spillways, the River periodically flooded into the lake, bringing fish, microorganisms and life-giving oxygen. Then, during cycles of drought, the lake levels receded, allowing organic material on the bottom to dry and be recycled as soil.

When the water rose again, the refreshed shorelines provided perfectly balanced spawning grounds, nurturing species all the way up the food chain. Those natural fluctuations can no longer occur, so the organic detritus on the floor of the lake actually steals oxygen from the water, which decreases the vitality of the entire ecosystem.

On one level, it sounds fairly straightforward, but building a consensus among those who love and use the lake has been difficult. For nearly three decades, Jim has worked to implement solutions that mimic nature, by periodically drawing down the lake and then allowing it to rise again. There have been some successes, he tells me, and many disappointments.

"People want the lake levels to remain consistent because they believe it is good for recreational business," he says with weariness in his voice, "They don't see the big picture. Some people," he continues, "see me as an outsider, even though I grew up here. It's hard to get them to listen."

There is determination in Jim's voice and manner and, when he calls these wetlands "paradise," his deep love and respect for his home is unmistakable. I am no biologist, but I do know people. Jim Johnson is a good man and Reelfoot Lake is blessed to have him as a friend.

When I tell my other new friends, my hosts Ruben and Tina Rodriquez, about Jim, they listen intently. "I have met Mr. Johnson only briefly," says Ruben, "but now I know that we must partner up with him in this effort." This journey is about connections. Every day, I see the amazing diversity of Americans in the way we speak, what we eat and how we spend our time – and right in the center of appreciating those differences, I am shown what is universal and connects us all.

High Cotton

I have no idea how this chunk of land known as "the Bootheel" came to belong to Missouri. The state's entire southern border is a straight line until these last 40 or so miles where it drops suddenly 50 miles southward and includes the land between the St. Francis and the Mississippi Rivers. When you see it on a map, it's easy to imagine a bunch of men arguing in a room filled with pipe smoke until someone finally says, "OK, fine – we'll give you this bit as well!"

Back then, the region was wild and swampy and not much prized. Today, after decades of swamp drainage, it is flat, cultivated and highly productive farmland. Peaches thrive in some areas and others favor watermelons, soybeans or rice, but here in the southernmost reaches of the Bootheel, cotton is king – and it is harvest time.

"The brittle, sharp-edged plants would surely have torn even the most calloused hands."

Cotton seems to be everywhere I look. It is waiting in the fields, smooshed into big round bales, encased in pastel wrappers and looking like giant nougat candy bars. It's blowing across the road in white, frothy waves and traveling the highway in the backs of semi-trucks. I've never seen cotton in these enormous rolls and my curiosity is piqued, so when the truck I am tailing turns off the highway, I follow to see if I can discover where it is bound. The answer comes quickly, as the truck and I turn into the L. Berry Cotton Gin at Holland, Missouri, just three miles north of the Arkansas border.

The truck takes its place in a line with its comrades and I turn toward a vast parking lot lined with orderly rows of bundled cotton. The yellow and green wrapped rolls are even bigger than they seemed from a distance – about eight feet in diameter, with the contents tightly compressed and the ends precisely sliced. In other rows, there are even larger, rectangular, plastic-topped bundles shaped like giant loaves of bread.

I walk the cotton-strewn aisles among them, picking up stray bolls, feeling the silky fibers and separating them to reveal the seeds buried within. A worker at the end of the row sees me and waves, smiling, but no one questions me.

There is a huge building where the gin must be and a smaller one that is clearly the office, which I decide to visit. The woman at the counter looks surprised when she sees me, but recovers graciously when I explain the journey of the raindrop. When I ask if anyone could spare a few moments to answer my questions, she leaves to ask and returns smiling broadly. Mr. Sonny Berry, she tells me, the owner of the company, is available and will see me.

Mr. Berry is a silver-haired Southern gentleman who seems not the least bit bothered by the interruption. As we walk, he tells me that his family has farmed this land for many generations, so he feels deeply rooted in the Bootheel. "The process of ginning cotton," he explains, "is basically the same as when Eli Whitney invented the first cotton gin in 1793. It's just easier and faster now."

The big round bundles of cotton are actually called "modules" and each one is the equivalent of four 500-pound bales. The equipment needed to handle the cotton in modules is the latest version of continually evolving machinery that streamlines cotton ginning. After the seeds and hulls are separated and packaged to be sold for other purposes, the cotton is cleaned and compressed into smaller bales. "It's all mechanized," he tells me, "and, like farming in general, requires much more equipment and much less manpower than in the past."

Cotton gins around here are running fourteen or more hours per day to keep up with the incoming cotton and ship it to market as quickly as possible. "It's a good year to be in the cotton business," he says, smiling. "The price of cotton is at an all-time high. The cotton industry suffered when synthetic fabrics were preferred, but that tide has turned and Delta cotton is the first choice for fine 'white goods'."

When I tour the gin at his invitation, there is an air of intensity as well as a tremendous amount of noise and dust, so I keep my camera safely zipped inside my jacket and make my visit brief. There is also, however, an air of cheerfulness and I am impressed that, in the midst of this hectic schedule, everyone I meet offers a smile and shows an easy willingness to pause and satisfy this wanderer's curiosity.

Back on the road, I pass through mile after mile of brown, dusty fields lying nearly naked, stripped of their bounty. Only random wisps of cotton cling to the dry, stubby plants and litter the ground like the morning after a party. Then, surprisingly, there is one field that seems to have evaded the harvester – its long rows are still frosted with clouds of puffy white. I pull over and walk an impossibly straight channel among them and wonder how the cotton bolls can be so pristinely *white* amidst the dust.

I pick a fat, fluffy one still partially protected by its sharp, prickly hull and imagine the slaves, sharecroppers and migrant workers who picked by hand what is now done by machine. The brittle, sharp-edged plants would surely have torn even the most calloused hands. Pictures come to mind of weary people stooped over the plants and dragging heavy bags of cotton, as they worked in the searing heat, harassed by insects, day after long day. It is barely imaginable.

Cotton has long been the linchpin of the South's economy and fields like this one form the backdrop to countless stories of wealth and horrific deprivation, of cruelty and kindness, of births, deaths, heroic acts and great loves. It seems perfect that on this day of transitioning into the South, I would be walking in a cotton field.

I tuck the rotund little icon behind my rearview mirror and it gleams in the sunlight like a beacon, leading me deeper into the complex, sometimes mysterious gumbo that is our American South.

The River Rat

When I tell Eric Golde of the Osceola, Arkansas, Chamber of Commerce about the 90-day journey of a raindrop, he quickly says, "There is someone here you've *got* to meet!" Two minutes after being introduced to Tommy Groves, I know that he was right.

Tommy is a soft-spoken, unassuming gentleman with kind eyes and a slow, boyish smile. When he speaks, I can feel the River in the cadence and the shape of his words. He seems to be saturated with the deep, familiar stillness of the River and the words of our conversation are less important than the energy of it. I feel myself gearing down a notch, relaxing and breathing a little deeper.

Tommy grew up in a three-room house on the bank of the Mississippi River. The little house, which stood on 6-foot stilts, was built before 1900, but it was made of cypress, so it didn't mind the wetness. "Nowadays," Tommy says smiling, "somebody would declare it a disaster when the floods come, but 50 years ago when I was a kid, it was just our way of life. The River was our home."

Every year when the water rose, they would be cut off from the mainland for a month or so. "Our house was four miles t'other side o' the levee. Daddy would take my sister and me in the boat in the mornin' to meet the school bus at the levee and get us again in the afternoon."

That brings to my mind mud, mess and inconvenience, but Tommy says, "Nah, we actually liked it when the water come up 'cause it meant the rabbits was easy to get. Lotsa times we woulda gone hungry if it weren't for the rabbits. We was poor folk, but we ate better'n lots of city folk did 'cause of the wildlife. That and the chickens my Mother kept in the yard. My Daddy rented ground and we raised cotton on it. We'd all work and take off for dinner from 11 till 1 and my Mother'd go 'cross the yard, grab a chicken, twist its head off, pick it and fry it up – and we'd have fried chicken, creamed potatoes and biscuits and gravy for dinner. It was a real good life."

There were a handful of other shotgun houses close by. "Sunday afternoons," he says, "the neighbors would all come over to our front yard and we'd play gospel music. Daddy played guitar and I played mandolin by the time I was seven or eight and we all sang. My sister especially was a real fine singer. It was the only entertainment we had. Yeah," he says again, "it sure was a good life."

In some ways, Tommy's life today looks quite different, but in the ways that matter, not much has changed. Both Tommy and his sister graduated from high school, then moved to town and became real estate agents and both have done well.

He's a man of many talents – he is a builder and has put up over 100 homes in Osceola, plus he's a plumber, an electrician and was even a policeman for a time. He's mostly retired now, but he still owns 50 rental houses which "make him a good living." He still plays music every weekend, except now it is in a theater in town that he owns. He still gets out on the River nearly every day, "Because I just feel good when I'm there."

He's a darned good fisherman, too, and in his spellbinding way, he tells me the tale of the 81-pound catfish he caught last fall. "I was in a real tug with him. It was such a battle that by the time I got him in, I was so tuckered out, I didn't even throw back out. I knew there was lots more big fish down in that hole and the next one might kill me!"

He usually doesn't keep them when they are that big, he says, "I just turn 'em back and let 'em live on.

They's like my brothers and sisters and I respect them a lot." This time, though, he knew a family with ten kids that needed food. "I gave that fish to them," he says, "and it fed them all for a week."

Finances improved for his parents, too, after those early hardscrabble years. "Daddy was a real good farmer," he tells me, "and he switched from plantin' cotton to soybeans at just the right time during the Carter years and got rich off it. Thing was, Daddy didn't trust banks," he continues, "'cause he'd lost $100 in one during the Depression, so he kept all his money in fruit jars and buried 'em. In 1984, when Daddy decided he was ready to quit farmin', I finally convinced him to put some money in the CD market and he trusted me to do that. Turned out, he had $300,000 in them fruit jars."

When I ask Tommy if he has traveled around much, he answers, "Nah – just only for our senior class trip and to take the family to Branson. I'm a River rat – and I just never could see anyplace I'd rather be than here. It's a real good life."

It's the natural time to say thank you and goodbye. I feel that and I feel the same thing that happens every time I leave the River – there is a subtle hanging-on because "it just feels good to be here." Thanks, Tommy.

"Nowadays, somebody would declare it a disaster when the floods come, but 50 years ago when I was a kid, it was just our way of life."

Another Piece of the Puzzle

After an all-night rain that finally broke the prolonged drought this region has endured, the clouds are separating and the trees are dressed in clean, shiny greens. The pavement glistens like black satin and the air feels brand new. A chorus of birdsong swells from the woods and a troupe of five deer bound across a meadow, following each other into the trees like ballet dancers exiting the stage. Happily, I left early so I can drive slowly and join in all this revelry.

My new friends in town have finagled an invitation for me to ride a tugboat working the busy River Port at Osceola, Arkansas. Although the terms are sometimes

Day 65 Osceola, Arkansas *October 27*

"Eddy Smith, a deckhand who seems to have the suction feet of a tree frog and the strength of Goliath, steadies me so firmly that my boots barely touch the ground."

confused, *tugboats* are essentially the smaller siblings of the much larger *towboats* like "The Phyllis" that I rode on the Upper Mississippi. The compact, yet powerful, tugs work where the tows cannot, maneuvering barges within harbors and shuttling them to and from the main channel.

The steep, rocky descent down the bank to the boat landing has been transformed into a slippery adventure by the wetness. Eddy Smith, a deckhand who seems to have the suction feet of a tree frog and the strength of Goliath, steadies me so firmly that my boots barely touch the ground and then welcomes me aboard "The Tommy Ross" with the panache of a cruise ship steward.

At his invitation, we visit the engine room first and, in spite of the protective earplugs he provides, the room full of throbbing, pounding metal is almost overwhelmingly intense. "She's got 1,200 horsepower," he yells proudly, as he checks meters and pours water into an opening.

We climb several flights of metal stairs to the sunny wheelhouse, where Captain Tommy Pinion welcomes me and then guides the boat across the harbor as we chat. I watch the squared-off bow, designed for pushing barges, plow flatly through the water and remember a conversation with another captain about driving such a boat, "It's tricky business without a barge in front," he had said. "If you go too fast, she'll just want to do a nose-dive." With practiced ease, Captain Tommy places the bow squarely against the end of a barge. "We're taking this empty one over to the Bunge Grain Elevator," he explains, "and they've got a loaded one ready for us."

I step out onto the catwalk to watch the two deck-hands below, as they attach the barge with a heavy rope and then step onto it and stride along the narrow ledge, as if it were a sidewalk. We chug across the harbor to the grain elevator, and the empty barge is then untied from the tug and attached to moorings on the shore by one end, while the other is left free. We then circle around to the loaded barge, and a deckhand lassos the heavy metal cleats mounted on its deck and pulls with his whole body.

The tug and the barge come together and the deck-hand wraps it tightly. As we back away with the loaded

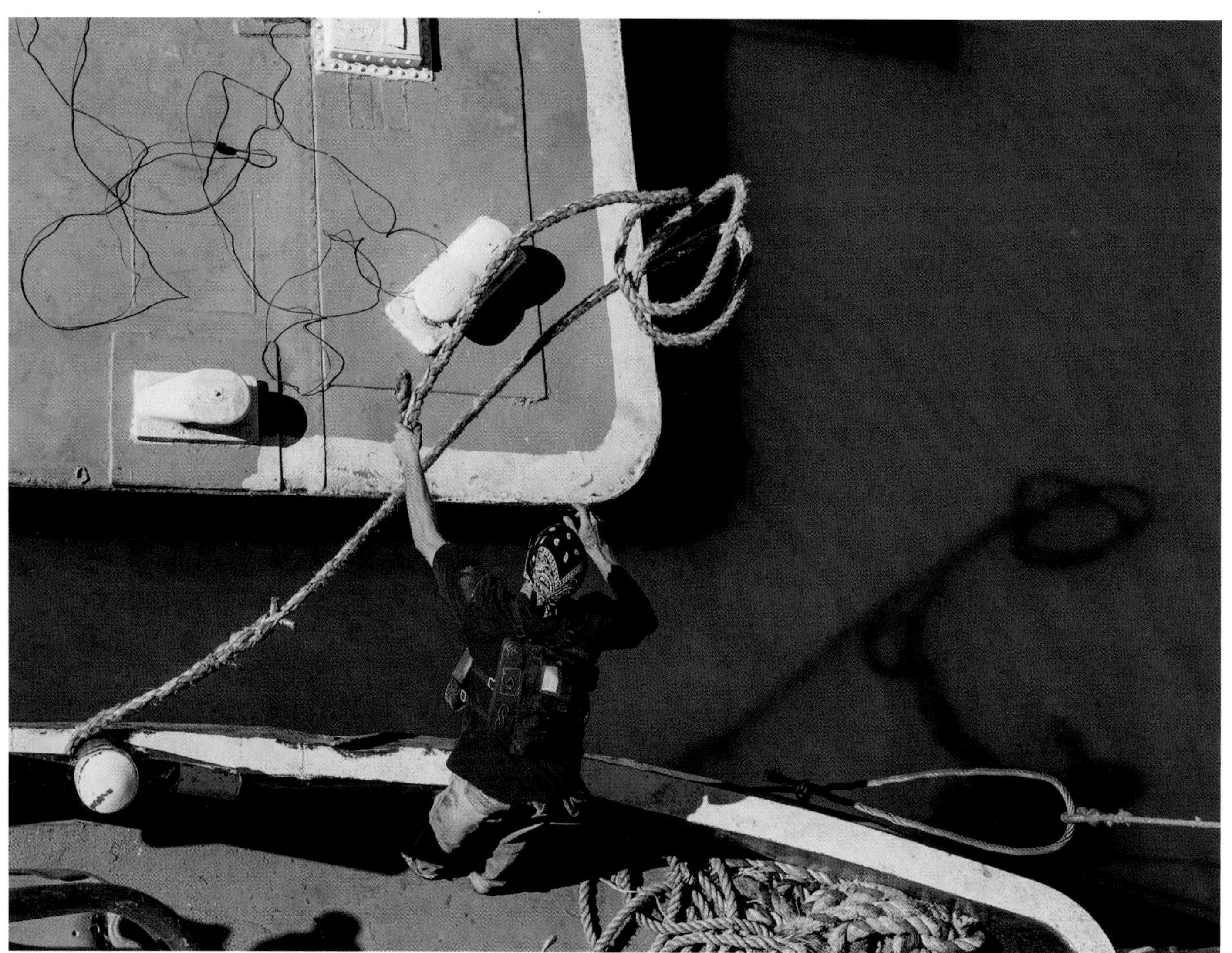

barge secured, I notice that the empty one that we just tied by only one end is being pivoted by the current, swinging around to land perfectly in place, underneath the loading arm of the grain elevator. We pull close and the deck hands step across onto the empty barge and walk along the top, lifting the heavy metal hatch doors and dropping them open with resounding clangs that must reverberate for miles.

Meanwhile, workers have appeared at the grain elevator and scaled a ladder to a platform far above us and are beginning the loading process. We push the loaded barge, which is now filled with 1,500 tons of rice, back across into the "slack water harbor," where it is tied up with others waiting for a towboat to take them downriver.

I watch the deckhands step lightly back onto the tug. Their work requires strength, plus the agility and balance of a mountain goat, and it is dangerous even on a perfect blue-sky morning like this one. The tugs, however, run 24 hours in all weather and all seasons. It's difficult to imagine anyone doing that work in the dark, in cold rain or freezing temperatures with the icy River below.

With this morning's ride, another piece of the puzzle that is the massive shipping industry made possible by the Mississippi, slides neatly into its place.

I seem to be the only one on this two-lane road to Memphis. The River flashes silver through a quick gap in the trees, and I think how mysterious she remains. I could do this journey ten more times and, although I would learn many more of her ways, there would be at least that much still undiscovered.

Chapter Seven: Deep in the South

"Around here, we don't much care what you do; we just want to know about it."

– Pal Foster, Clarksdale, Mississippi

Minding My Business

Highway 61, which generally follows the course of the Mississippi River from Minnesota to Louisiana, is often designated as the Great River Road and is now almost as familiar to me as the River itself. It stretches out in front of me now, uninterrupted by crossroads or curves and invites me to put the car on cruise and stretch myself out as well.

The morning is coming on slowly – even the birds are sleeping late. The moisture-laden air veils the world like gossamer and the sun's first slanting rays give it depth and density. There is something intimate and private about this kind of morning that, when added to the sense of freedom that such wide-open spaces bring, results in one very happy woman.

I'm tracing the eastern border of central Arkansas and when I take the next bridge across the Mississippi, I will be delivered smack into the heart of Memphis, Tennessee. I've dipped in and out of this city before

Day 66 Memphis, Tennessee *October 28*

and, each time, come away with an impression based on a single aspect. Like the Indian parable of the blind men, however, who try to describe an elephant after touching only its tail or its trunk, Memphis is mostly an undiscovered entity. Somehow, these thoughts lead me to the notion that I should prioritize possibilities and make a plan for my two days in the city.

I have visited the National Civil Rights Museum in Memphis, at the site of the Lorraine Motel, and stared up at the balcony seared into our collective memory as the place where Dr. Martin Luther King, Jr.'s life was cut short. Inside, I sat beside the likeness of Mrs. Rosa Parks on a Montgomery city bus and felt the driver's contempt, as he fiercely demands that she move to the back. I've spent hours among the photos and videos, at once heartbreaking and inspiring, showing the hatred and fear of that dark time and the astonishing courage of those who fought for change.

I have been on nocturnal Beale Street at the moment when dusk awakens it. On cue, clutches of people appear, take up their plastic cups of beer and fall in for the nightly promenade. Neon lights, pitching soul food and barbeque, throw green, red and blue shadows on their faces. Hawkers in doorways cajole, tease and tantalize with practiced banter in husky voices. Street performers gather their audiences, building anticipation with sneak previews. Strains of rock and roll, jazz and blues shimmer through the spicy, smoky air like heat waves rising from the sidewalk. When the cast is assembled, the nightly party begins in earnest.

I have also followed the celebrated Peabody Ducks as they waddle off to bed. After a day of paddling around the travertine marble fountain in the sumptuous Peabody Hotel lobby, the red-jacketed Duckmaster appears. Once the red carpet has been rolled out, the four hens and a drake hop out, shake their tail feathers and, ignoring the gaggle of fans snapping photos, march in a line toward the elevator. On the rooftop, they will retire to the Royal Duck Palace until the ritual is reversed in the morning.

"As the behemoth looms closer, my spine tingles and my hold on the paddle becomes a white-knuckled death grip."

This time, I think, first up must be Mud Island and the acclaimed Mississippi River Museum. I've wanted to visit and, especially, to see the five-block long scale model of the Lower Mississippi River, for years. And, I've never been to Elvis Presley's Graceland, so it seems time to visit that icon of Memphis and rock and roll. There is also the intriguing Center for Southern Folklore, which is dedicated to preserving the distinctive culture of the Mississippi Delta. Finally, at some point, there are some River-loving "Memphians" that I am looking forward to meeting who have already been helpful and welcoming.

The latter, it turns out, is where I begin. Diana Threadgill is the Executive Director of the Mississippi River Corridor of Tennessee. When I arrive, she immediately invites me to lunch with her and her colleague, Glenn Cox. It doesn't take long to feel their dedication and, as we talk, the effectiveness of their organization is also obvious. It's easy enough to love this River, but gathering people together and blending their disparate visions into a cogent plan for its care, as they are doing, is not. They are committed friends to the River.

It's also easy to see why Diana is good at her job. She's a competent, high-energy dynamo whose dry sense of humor sneaks in on her easy Tennessee cadence and keeps me in constant anticipation of the next, inevitable, chuckle. By the end of lunch, it's like being with an old friend. Before I know it, we have visited her hairdresser to have my unruly locks trimmed, and we are exploring Memphis' neighborhoods, laughing all the way.

At the Riverfront, Diana takes me to a place I would almost certainly never have gone on my own – the National Ornamental Metal Museum. The elaborate 16-foot tall gate marking the entrance is set with 360 rosettes, each one a distinctive expression of a different metal artist.

Beyond it, a path winds through a sculpture garden of surprises. It's not an art form I am familiar with and some pieces – like the clothesline hung with tapestries seemingly flapping the breeze – are so lifelike and delicate that it's hard to believe they are made of metal. Inside the Museum, an impressive collection traces metal arts through five centuries and gives me a new appreciation for this medium.

Even more intriguing, though, is the Blacksmith Shop out back. A wall of noise and gritty intensity meets us at the door, but, as we step inside, a fresh-faced, smiling young woman greets us. She is Holly Fisher, an Artist-in-Residence who has moved from her home in Iowa to hone her skills and further her craft at this renowned institution. In her leather apron and denim work shirt, with her hair safely tucked into a bandana and hands smudged with metal gray, she looks to be completely in her element. As she shows us her current project, a hefty "bracelet for a giant," she explains a little about her technique.

When Holly hears about my project, she invites me back into her fiery workspace to watch. After she outfits me with safety glasses and earplugs, I follow her. Hammers clang, fires roar, machines thump and bang and music blares. It is sensory overload for me and, for a minute, I freeze. I'm sure my expression must be goggle-eyed and comical, but Holly smiles serenely, settles into her work and is soon as lost in it as a plein air painter in a meadow.

I start shooting, dancing around her as she moves, and, as I do, the intensity of it all fades into the background, and I'm lost in my own creative moment. Conversation between us is impossible and unnecessary, but we share a playful and wordless connection that leaves us both grinning.

The day has nearly vanished when Diana says suddenly, "Oh, my Gosh! You *need* to meet my friend, Joe Royer! I am calling him right now!" She does and, before I can say, "Serendipity," Joe and I have made a plan to meet in the morning.

Whirls of mist float above the River as Joe and I settle into his 22-foot sea kayak. We paddle out of the small harbor and turn into the vast, open River. The Mississippi is a mile wide here and sitting at surface-level, with just inches of boat on either side, brings an exquisite, heart-clutching awareness of its power.

"The River has a reputation for being dangerous," Joe says reassuringly from the stern, "but, if you respect it and learn the proper skills, it is safe and fun." Joe has

done this hundreds of times and his comfort is contagious, so I soon relax into the rhythm of our paddling. The kayak slices silently through the current and the soft morning, and of all the ways that I have been with and on this River, I have never felt such a sublime *intimacy* with it.

I hear the familiar moan of a barge horn, just before I see it coming around a bend. From this perspective, the thing looks *colossal* and it seems to be racing toward us at breakneck speed! I wait for Joe to maneuver us closer to shore, but he paddles on at the same tranquil pace.

As the behemoth looms closer, my spine tingles and my hold on the paddle becomes a white-knuckled death grip. It comes even with us and churns past us and when I see the wake angling out from behind, it looks like a freaking *tsunami*! I resist glancing back at Joe or saying anything – there is no way he is unaware of it. It rolls toward us and I brace for it. Joe turns us slightly into it and…we slide up and over it with only a gentle rise and fall. It is almost nothing. I nearly laugh out loud with relief and embarrassment. If Joe has noticed my greenhorn anxiety, he kindly makes no comment and we paddle onward.

With my heartbeat back to normal, we glide beneath the Hernando de Soto Bridge. Above us are six lanes of morning rush hour traffic on Interstate 40. I think about the hundreds of commuters in those streams of vehicles, and the contrast between their experience in this moment and my own is so profound that it brings a rush of emotion. Sometimes, I am still incredulous at my good fortune to be making this journey.

Back on the Great River Road, leaving Tennessee behind as I cross into Mississippi, I remember my agenda for Memphis. Not one bit of it happened. It seems I needed to be reminded not to mess with Serendipity's business.

In the Presence of Greatness

Clarksdale, Mississippi, greets you like an old hound lying in the Delta sun, with an almost imperceptible lifting of one eyelid. If you're in a hurry, you might blow on by, barely noticing one more threadbare, dusty Delta town. It's as if you have to earn the right to *really* see Clarksdale, by just hangin' a while and letting it come to you in its own time and its own way.

Tommy Polk, whom I will meet downriver in Natchez, is a songwriter whose music has been recorded by such artists as Martina McBride and Crystal Gayle. He owns a guesthouse in Clarksdale called "The Big Pink," where I am graciously invited to stay. "Pal" (short for Palmer) Foster, manager of the guesthouse, welcomes me into the foyer of the pink Victorian home, where Elvis sneers down from atop a scarf-draped grandfather clock. He's there, Pal tells me, because the previous owner of the home (whose colorful life story could apparently be a book unto itself) dated "The King" for a few months.

We pass through the parlor and the dining room, which are furnished in a playful mix of gorgeous antiques and funky, quirky accessories, to an interior courtyard where wooden duck decoys float in an elaborate, cascading fountain. Behind that is a tightly spiraled staircase, which we ascend to a tiny balcony and "The Stella," which will be my home for two nights.

"Your room is named in homage to Stella of *A Streetcar Named Desire*," says Pal, "because Tennessee Williams lived in Clarksdale." Eudora Welty and John Faulkner lived here as well, he says, and there are tales of the three literary legends spending long evenings "trying to drink each other under the table."

Pal, like most Southerners, is a natural storyteller and, once he sees that I am an eager audience, he regales me with tale after tale of his hometown's kaleidoscope of characters, past and present. As he explains with a sly grin, "Around here, we don't much care *what* you do; we just want to know about it."

If you're a fan of the Delta Blues, you likely know about Clarksdale – many say it's where it all began. Legend has it that the intersection of Highways 61 and 49, at the edge of town, is the spot made famous by Robert Johnson's 1930s classic, "Cross Road Blues," and where, it is claimed, he sold his soul to the devil in exchange for his astonishing skill on the guitar. Even if you are not familiar with this rich, sultry, soul-stirring, hip-grinding music, you will likely recognize a few of the names of the Blues greats who have lived and made music here, like Muddy Waters, John Lee Hooker, Son House and W.C. Handy.

Music is, in fact, everywhere – in juke joints and Blues clubs and even on the sidewalk at the Saturday morning farmers' market, where a multi-generational trio of musicians plays for shoppers and, clearly, for themselves.

I watch a talented boy of about twelve passionately complete a drum solo and, as the other musicians rejoin him, something unfolds that shows me how talent is allowed to flourish here. A little guy of perhaps three, barely tall enough to reach the cymbals with his sticks, but serious about making music with them, steps up and begins to bang away, following his own beat. No one stops him – the others smile and keep playing. That's how it happens.

Morgan Freeman, one of my favorite actors, lives not far away and is nurturing the current crop of blues artists at his Clarksdale juke joint, "Ground Zero" (named *before* 2001). In fact, as Clarksdale begins to show itself to me, there is a growing sense that this place fairly oozes with creative energy being expressed in every possible way. It makes one want to drink plenty of tap water or suck in great gulps of the earthy-smelling air or absorb it in whatever way it is done. I *love* the story of Freeman's answer to a talk show host's question, "Why in the world would you choose to live in Mississippi? Because I can," he said.

After hearing from three different people, "You really

should meet John Ruskey," I wander into his shop, the Quapaw Canoe Company, to see if that is possible. I find him out back, packing gear and canoes and surrounded by a troupe of chattering, laughing Boy Scouts preparing for a river adventure on the Mississippi. In the midst of all the hubbub, John greets me with a slow, easy smile and sparkly eyes and pauses to tell me about his work.

For more than twenty years, John has been paddling the Mississippi and making it possible for others to do so. He leads expeditions, teaches classes and workshops and makes canoes, ranging from dugouts to the 22-foot wooden slat canoe being loaded up at the moment. Honestly, the wood and workmanship of this boat are so elegant, it looks more like a piece of fine furniture than something you would fill with Boy Scouts and put in the Mississippi.

As he gathers the boys and gives their first instructions, I have a sense of how much they will learn about canoeing, about the River and the life it supports – and much more. I even have a (fleeting) moment of wishing I were going along! I do see, somewhere in my future, a trip back to town for a quieter float on the River with John. Although I hear none of it from him, I learn later that, in true Clarksdale style, John is also a gifted musician, painter and writer.

Finally, with kudos to the pure magic of Serendipity, I am granted an opportunity to meet Mr. Marshall Bouldin, III. Mr. Bouldin is a nationally-known portrait artist whose work is found in major museums and in the private collections of many powerful and famous individuals. It's an illustrious career that he has enjoyed for most of his 87 years, yet as impressive as that is, it is not what makes the experience of meeting him so potent.

My new friend, Pal, has known him a lifetime and says it still feels like "an audience with the Pope" when he visits. Immediately when we are introduced, I feel such a strong presence about him, such a sense of wisdom and goodness that I want only to be quiet and listen.

He talks about art – what it is and what it is not

"I'll get a letter every few months from someone I painted 20, 30 or 40 years ago, telling me how much pleasure the painting has given them…"

– and how he is always striving toward that perfect balance between an actual representation of the person and that ungraspable quality that stops you and *says something* to you about that person. He gets up every morning, excited to get to work and see what problems or ideas will appear, always hoping to do something new or better or different and always knowing it isn't something within his power to do. "It ain't me," he says. "I'm just here playing, doing what I enjoy, what I think God wants me to do. I'm the most fortunate man in the world."

He speaks of sometimes feeling selfish because, "…mostly I just want to stay here and paint. But, you know," he continues, as tears moisten his eyes, "I'll get a letter every few months from someone I painted 20, 30 or 40 years ago, telling me how much pleasure the painting has given them – and then I know this is what God wants me to do."

He never realized he was getting old, he tells me, until last year when he had a fall and his injury made it difficult to work as he always had. When the motion of stepping forward to paint and then backward to see the result was challenging, he invented a moving easel that he can push away with his foot and pull back with a cord, while he paints from a sitting position. He has plans to retire, he says, on his 101st birthday.

I tell him that last night Pal loaned me the beautiful book printed by the Mississippi Museum of Art, chronicling his life and work and he tells me, with emotion in his voice, how his son worked with the museum to create it and presented it to him as a surprise.

Then, I find myself telling him this, "You, know, I have been on the road now for 68 days and, although it is wonderful, it is a non-stop marathon of long and full days. I noticed yesterday that I was weary and that, if I wasn't careful, I could begin to skate a little, to not give it all I have every day. Reading your book last night and being with you today has renewed and inspired me and reminded me that my only job is to say thank you for this moment and to keep doing what it seems I am meant to do. I cannot thank you enough."

Now, both of us are smiling through moist eyes and it is time to go.

Basking in Sunshine

"You just get yourself on over here, little one," Sonny says with his usual mix of gruffness and tenderness. Now…I have been 5'10" tall since my sixteenth birthday, so that's not something I'm often called, which makes it all the more endearing.

I'm backtracking, heading north from Clarksdale to cross the River at Helena, Arkansas, to meet Sonny for Sunday dinner after mass. I'm on a desolate stretch of road through flatter-than-flat Delta crop land, where every tree was long ago sacrificed to the plow, so the mind is free to roam. I am remembering how Sonny and I met.

I was tired, damp and chilled to the bone when I went in search of a hot meal at the end of a dreary, and mostly unsuccessful, day of shooting for a magazine assignment. The café in downtown Helena was warm and welcoming and I sat huddled in my coat, drinking hot tea and reading the flier I had picked up at the door. It was promoting an upcoming Blues event and a short bio at the bottom described the emcee, "Sunshine" Sonny Payne.

Sonny Payne, it said, is one of Helena's own and a legend in the Blues world. He is the host of the King Biscuit Time Radio Show, the longest running Blues radio program in the world and he has been honored for his work in many ways, including being inducted into the Blues Hall of Fame. He annually emcees the King Biscuit Blues Festival, which brings an unimaginable 100,000 fans to this quiet town of 6,000.

I was intrigued, so I asked my waiter if he knew him. "Sure do," he said with a grin. "He comes in here every night. As a matter of fact, that's his table right next to you and he should be here any minute. Would you like to meet him?" (Ah, sweet Serendipity!)

I liked Sonny when I saw him come in the door and by the end of dinner, I was smitten by his quick wit and his mischievous, if infrequent, smile. When he invited me to visit him in the morning at the studio of KFFA Radio, I hesitated not a second.

The Delta Cultural Center, where the studio is housed, is a must-see museum for Blues fans and anyone interested in the music and the culture of the Delta. With Sonny as my guide, every exhibit sprang to life with anecdotes about his friends, the Blues greats of the past seven decades. He told me about coming to work at the radio station in 1942, at the age of seventeen, as a janitor and errand boy. After reading a few on-air commercials (without permission) on a day when the announcer was absent, a legendary career was born. Today, 16,000 shows later, King Biscuit Time is streamed via the internet to Blues fans all over the world.

It was a quiet morning in the museum and not yet time to go on-air, so Sonny leaned on the glass partition surrounding the broadcast booth and beguiled me with tales of his 85 amazing years. When he began to talk about his wife, Josephine, the love of his life, his voice grew soft and choked with emotion. Josephine had passed away a few years ago and, when he leaned

" He has a deadpan way of slipping in a little joke, just to see if you will catch it. "

Day 69 Helena, Arkansas *October 31*

a little closer and told me of their last moments together, the connection and trust between us seemed to have been created long ago. I treasure the gift of that moment.

When I left, he made me promise "to keep love in my heart and to come back to see him." So, there was never any doubt that I would visit Sonny on this journey.

As we walk into the restaurant, virtually everyone there calls out a greeting to him. He gives little nods or waves, but no smiles. Sonny tries to be crotchety, but he is really too sweet to pull it off. He grumbles about a few things as we settle in, but he can't squelch the smiles that shine from his eyes, no matter what his mouth is doing. He has a deadpan way of slipping in a little joke, just to see if you will catch it. If you do, you are granted a quick, but brilliant, smile that warms you like the sun suddenly bursting through clouds.

He fusses at me for not making it to the King Biscuit Blues Festival (again!) and tells me that his old friend, B.B. King, came this year. They had a ride in B.B.'s bus and reminisced about old times, while a film crew recorded it.

We catch each other up over lunch and then go back to his house, because he wants to show me some pictures. With the photos to cue him, the stories roll like the River and I am again astounded at his recall of names, dates and details. I eat up his stories like candy.

Once I have put next year's festival dates on my calendar, it is time to go. He makes me promise to call when I get home, so he knows I made it safely.

Shine on, Sonny! I'll see you next time.

Tales of a Lake and the Village That Spoons It

Unlike the Upper Mississippi, where steep bluffs are evidence that the River has been carving away the bedrock of that same channel for millennia, the nature of the Lower Mississippi is to constantly redesign itself. When you see its swerving, looping course on a map, it seems that if one could stretch it out straight, it might cover three or four times the distance that it does now.

The soft soil through which the Lower Mississippi now courses was actually brought here by the River from the interior of the continent, over many thousands of years. In ancient times, the Gulf of Mexico extended much farther north, into the area now known as the Bootheel of Missouri, which meant that the River ended there. The natural action of the River is to drop its load of sediment where it ends, gradually building land. As areas become built up enough that marshes and, eventually, trees appear, the River turns away to find a path of less resistance. In this way, it continually swerves back and forth on its journey to sea level.

Sometimes, after creating a loop in this way, the River will take the shortcut, cutting off the loop and leaving behind an oxbow lake. The Mississippi has created many such graceful, arching lakes and the largest in North America is Lake Chicot (pronounced CHEE-ko) in southernmost Arkansas, just twenty miles north of the Louisiana border. Its 5,300 acres of clear water lie within a shapely letter "C" that was cut off from the mother River more than 600 years ago.

Snugged against the broad, curved back of Lake Chicot is the town of Lake Village, where my current home takes its place on the ever-surprising list of unique places I have slept. As a guest at the Pecan Grove RV Park, I am staying in a refurbished sharecropper's cabin, surrounded by a century-old pecan grove.

"When you hear Miss Ella speak in that tone of voice, there is nothing to say except, 'Yes, Ma'am,' no matter who you are."

As I start to discover the town and its people, chapters of Lake Chicot's colorful history appear like squares in a patchwork quilt. There's the story of Hernando de Soto's rather inglorious end. In 1541, de Soto was among the first Europeans to see and cross the Mississippi River. It was his belief that if the native people he encountered could become convinced that he was actually an immortal sun god, they would acquiesce to his demands without conflict. To that end, he and his men did everything they could to foster that illusion.

In 1542, after exploring as far west as what is now Texas, de Soto and company returned to the Mississippi River. While camped just north of here, de Soto contracted a fever and died. Hoping to conceal the death and perpetuate the hoax of immortality, it is said that his men wrapped the body in sand-filled blankets and slid him into Lake Chicot.

Then there's the story of a moonlit evening in April of 1923, when Charles Lindbergh, who feels like an old friend to me after my time in Little Falls, Minnesota, made his historic, first-ever, night flight here. It was four years before the trans-Atlantic flight that would make him internationally famous, when Lindbergh put his mail plane down in a field beside the lake.

The owner of a nearby inn offered hospitality and, after dinner, the two men watched a full moon appear in a gloriously clear evening. Lindbergh looked at the softly illumined landscape and surprised his host with an invitation for a ride. The two soared over Lake Chicot, the Mississippi River and the surrounding landscape in the moonlight, and the innkeeper said it was the most enjoyable time of his life. "What his reaction would have been," Lindbergh said later, "had he known that I had never flown after dark before, is a matter of speculation."

Then comes the story of Sunnyside Plantation. In the years before the Civil War, the rich, alluvial soil of this region was primarily held in huge parcels by profitable cotton plantations that depended upon the labor of thousands of slaves. In fact, in 1850 in Chicot County alone, 145 white families owned a total of nearly 4,000 slaves. Sunnyside Plantation, situated on the extremely fertile ground between the lake and the River, was the largest and richest of all.

In the aftermath of the Civil War, plantation owners all over the South struggled to rebuild while dealing with a massive labor shortage and low cotton prices. At Sunnyside, the troubles were further compounded by a devastating flood in 1882. As a result, ownership of the plantation was taken over by a New York banker, Austin Corbin, who devised a new plan for acquiring laborers. Corbin formed a partnership with the mayor of Rome, Don Emanuele Ruspoli, to recruit Italian families.

Disillusioned with the poverty and political unrest in their own country, and lured by the promise of a 12 ½-acre plot in a resplendent land of plenty, 100 Italian families immigrated to the U.S. to work in Sunnyside's cotton fields. In 1895, they arrived in a new land with few possessions, but very high hopes.

Their utopian dreams disintegrated quickly. They lacked the knowledge and the tools to grow the unfamiliar crop of cotton, and there were language barriers with their supervisors. They were tormented by hordes of mosquitoes, and the Delta's oppressive heat and humidity were a great hardship for people accustomed to a mild Mediterranean climate. Malaria and other illnesses, caused by an unsanitary water supply, ravaged the colony and medical care was scarce. The "extra work" that had been promised, to carry them through until their crops could be harvested, did not materialize. They were forced, as a result, to buy supplies from the company store at exorbitant prices and inflated interest rates, so most fell quickly and deeply into debt.

Three years after arriving, nearly half the beleaguered colony decided to follow the plantation's resident priest, Father Pietro Bandini, to the Ozarks in northwest Arkansas to begin again, in a village they named Tontitown. For those who stayed behind, their

lives slowly improved and today, their descendants make up a large, vibrant and cohesive Italian American community in Lake Village.

When I am told that there are two women considered matriarchs in town, one from the African American community and one from the Italian American, I know that I would like to meet them both.

When Mrs. Ella Edwards welcomes me into her comfortable home, the first thing I see is a dining table big enough to seat sixteen or so and walls nearly covered with smiling faces.

"That's my family," she says chuckling. "They're all pictures of my six kids, sixteen grandchildren, forty-five great-grandchildren and five great-greats. A whole bunch of 'em will be here for Thanksgiving," she continues. "I'll be cookin' for a week gettin' ready." When I ask if many of them live close enough to come often, she says, "Yep – they come, I spoil 'em and they go."

"Miss Ella," as she is known in the respectful way of Southerners, came to Lake Village as a 15-year-old bride from her hometown of Eudora, fifteen miles south of here. When her husband passed away several years ago, they had been married for more than 60 years. After raising her own children, she also raised a grandchild and a great-grandchild and, she says, they have kept her young.

Miss Ella speaks then about the importance of teaching young people respect, and says she's not afraid to remind those who aren't so young, either, if they need it. She stopped a choir practice once, and asked the director for a moment to speak. "This is the Lord's House," she said, "and you got no business comin' in here with pants on and lookin' half undressed. You got to show some respect and come in here *dressed* for the Lord's House." Things changed after that. When you hear Miss Ella speak in *that* tone of voice, there is nothing to say except, "Yes, Ma'am," no matter who you are.

When she talks about life in Lake Village, she says, "It's a great place to live if you're retired, but the young folks all have to go away to get jobs. There just ain't none here. It's peaceful," she continues. "There's 2,500 people here and 60 percent are African Americans and then there's the Italians, the Hispanics and a Jewish community and others too. We all get along pretty well. Even during the '60s, when there was trouble all over, it stayed pretty quiet here."

Then she says again, "It's all about respect," and as I look at her no-nonsense expression with a tiny hint of a smile, I have the feeling that Miss Ella has more than a little influence on the way people treat one another in Lake Village.

Mrs. Libby Borgognoni manages the finances of their family's farm from her office in town. When she welcomes me there, she greets me with, "Oh my! It's such a shame you *just missed* being here for our annual spaghetti dinner!" Sadly, a few days ago, the women of Our Lady of the Lake Catholic Church served up nearly 3,000 plates of made-from-scratch pasta and homemade sauce – *darn!*

Miss Libby's great-great-grandparents were among that first group of Italian immigrants to arrive in 1895. There is pride and admiration in her voice as she speaks about their hardship, courage and determination. Even for Miss Libby's own parents, life was still tough, but they had what mattered. "When I was a child," she says, "we were very, very poor – but we had a beautiful, happy life."

Because she was often needed to work in the cotton field, she was only able to attend school when it rained or the field was dormant, but, because she was bright and worked hard, she was able to keep up. The family was so self-sufficient and resourceful that they needed to buy only salt, pepper, sugar and flour – and the flour sacks were reused and made into clothing. They gathered berries and grew peaches, apricots, pears, eggplant, peppers and fava beans.

"We made our own wine and we raised hogs," she continues, "and we used every bit of that pig except his hair. We made prosciutto and salsiccia, which is a wonderful sausage that uses the intestines for casing." In her smooth and precise Southern speech that stretches one syllable words into three, she says, "Maybe best of all…when it was time to butcher a hog, we'd cut his throat, hang him upside down and drain the blood. Then we'd bake that blood into a blood pie and *that* was just divine!"

"It really was a beautiful way to live," she says in a voice that makes the words dance. "We lived with my grandmother and there was always lots of other family around, and we kids made our own fun with whatever we could find." Weddings, she says, were huge celebrations that went on for two or three days with music, singing, dancing, wine and feasting.

When she and her husband, Tony, married, they began with nothing. But, because they worked hard, she says, while raising their five children, and because Tony loves the land and is one of the best farmers anywhere around, they have done well. They saved carefully and each time they had enough for a down payment, they would buy a piece of land until, eventually, they were farming 8,000 acres in cotton, wheat, rice and soybeans, plus raising cattle and hogs. As they always have, they still go into the fields together every evening after dinner, so Tony can plan the next day's work. They are a team, she says.

When it's time to leave, Miss Libby gives me a cookbook of authentic Italian recipes, compiled by the women of the Altar Society at Our Lady of the Lake Church. When I peek at a few, they seem long and complex and I comment that they look a mite intimidating. "Oh no," she says laughing, "you could do it. You just give it a try!" That, I would bet, might fairly well summarize how Libby Borgognoni handles most things in life.

Dusk crawls in under the pecan trees and closes in on my little sharecropper's cabin. I think about all those who have passed time on this front stoop, looking out at land so flat that it's hard to imagine even the slightest grade toward the level of the sea. Insects tune up and a field mouse scurries under the porch. I sip tea, and watch the stories I've been told drift into symmetries and patterns and stitch themselves together. The moment is perfect.

Sweet Home

I didn't grow up in the Delta, nor have I ever lived here and yet, somehow, it always feels like home. It's all unaccountably familiar – cheese grits, hot tamales and sweet tea, the heavy air, the raspy, smoky sound of the Blues, and even the gigantic and seemingly invincible palmetto bugs. Mostly, though, it's the people.

It's the way everyone knows your business, and how the telling of it is fine entertainment. It's the way quirks and eccentricities are not just accepted, but appreciated for their enhancement of a good story, like the spice in the stew. It's something in their eyes that draws you in and makes you feel seen and heard and recognized.

I'm a little tired as I roll into Greenville, Mississippi. I don't know anyone here and I don't know much about the town. I'm planning a quiet evening in my hotel room, regrouping, eating microwaved soup and calling it a night. After I call home, I decide on just one more phone call – to a friend of a friend who sometimes lives in Greenville – Eden Brent, a talented Blues singer and pianist. She calls me back immediately and says she is in Chicago on tour, but we have a hilarious conversation (she's a *hoot*!). Then she says, "You have just *got* to meet my Daddy! I'm going to call him right now."

Ten minutes later, there is this message from the front desk, "Mr. Howard Brent was just here. He said to say that you are invited to a party at Doe's Eat Place and he will be back to pick you up at 6:45." Well, alright then – I guess I'll shower.

It's a little frame building in a rough part of town, with no parking to speak of, so Doe's hires an off-duty policeman to watch over people and direct traffic. On one side of the front room, walls are covered with postcards and photos of happy customers. On the other, "Baby Doe" stands at the fiery broiler, tending massive steaks and waving his tongs in greeting, as people stream in and call out to him. Baby Doe, I am told, took over from his Daddy, "Doe Junior," who replaced his Daddy, "Big Doe," who started it all in 1941.

Next, we squeeze behind a grandmotherly woman in the kitchen making salads, although it's hard to imagine how the salads ever get finished, because she stops continually to exclaim over the next person through the door and throw her arms wide to hug them.

Then, it's past the huge stove with five cast iron skillets of sizzling french fries in various stages of brownness, and into the dining room. We thread our way through groups of noisy, laughing people at tables covered with a hodgepodge of well-used vinyl tablecloths, toward the small party room at the back.

The party is in honor of a local doctor, although it is never quite clear to me if the occasion is retirement, birthday or just an excuse to have a party. The room is already crowded, but guests pour in, leaving bottles of wine and liquor on the card table by the door and greeting the doctor, before diving into the river of hugs and conversations. I am introduced and then gathered up and swept away.

Conversation is an art form in the South, a bit like music. When a friend joins a group, he or she is granted the stage for a time and allowed a brief solo, before the others resume. Then, it rises up again, from every direction, somehow keeping the rhythm even when they run over each other, until it is someone else's turn for a solo. I am swirled around the room, passed from one melodic teller of tales to the next.

It feels like the most natural thing in the world to pass the evening in this company of friends. There are lots of ways to understand "home."

"Baby Doe took over from his Daddy, 'Doe Junior,' who replaced his Daddy, 'Big Doe,' who started it all in 1941."

A Circle Completed

I am the first visitor of the day at Winterville Mounds State Park, just north of Greenville. "Your timing is perfect," says a staff member, as she unlocks the Visitors Center. "You should have time to walk out to the mounds before the school kids get here. It's Native American Days," she says grinning, "and they will be coming by the busloads."

I take her advice and climb the 55-foot tall Temple Mound while all is quiet. Like other mound sites I have visited along the River, this was built by people of the Mississippian Culture more than 1,000 years ago. Although archeologists have learned much about the ways of these ancient people, I am fascinated by the mysteries that remain. I sit for a few minutes in the quiet and feel, as I have in other sites like this, the strong sense of history and presence that resides here. Then, a quick tour of the exhibits of artifacts and pottery before the quiet is obliterated.

"The doors of the yellow bus open and kids burst out like shaken soda from a can and swarm in every direction."

The doors of the yellow bus open and kids burst out like shaken soda from a can and swarm in every direction. A second and third bus pull close behind, each releasing its cargo of high-decibel, high-energy kids, and the park is alive with their exuberance. Some climb the mounds and a few tour the museum, but most head toward the Native people in colorful regalia that are waiting for them under the trees.

A circle forms around a man playing his flute. When he finishes, he invites them to sit, and tells them about the voice of the flute and its significance in his culture. Then he plays again, a haunting, soaring tune that draws more kids to quietly join the circle. It stills them, quiets the jitters in their legs, and they seem captivated.

He has their full attention now as he explains his regalia, how it was made and what it symbolizes. "Many of the feathers," he says, "were taken from birds killed on the road." There are a few, "eeews," with that, but when he says, "That is a way of giving them life again," all is quiet. Afterwards, the kids crowd around him with questions. When they move on, I introduce myself and, at his invitation, we move to a picnic table under a tree.

He is Cocoa Cappel, he tells me, a full-blooded Houma and a fireman in New Orleans. He makes time in a busy life, he says, to share his culture in order to help preserve it and to promote understanding. Then he talks about New Orleans, and how profoundly it has been changed since Hurricane Katrina. "Things like that bring out the best and the very worst in people," he says, and tells me about being shot at while trying to rescue stranded people during that awful time.

When I ask about his name, Cocoa, he grins a little sheepishly. "Well, not many people know this story," he says, "but…I was raised by my grandmother and she had a little dog named Cocoa. When I was very small, every time she called the dog, I would also come running, so she named me Cocoa too."

As we start to say our goodbyes, Cocoa invites me to call him when I get to New Orleans, and I promise to try. Then, suddenly, I remember something! Underneath my front seat is a bag of tobacco! It has been there for 1,200 miles and many weeks, waiting for this moment.

Remember the meeting with the Ojibwe man in northern Minnesota? I had been embarrassed then, that I hadn't known to come prepared with a traditional gift of tobacco or rice. Now, I tell Cocoa the story of that meeting and ask if he will accept the gift that I have been carrying. He would be honored, he says, and I hurry to my car.

It's a small, simple thing, that doesn't feel small at all. Cocoa seems as pleased to receive it as I am to give it, and a beautiful circle has been completed.

Eyes

I have no clue where I am. Since I left Greenville this morning, I have taken the next road that beckons without any notice of its name or direction.

A cloudless but hazy sky meets the horizon in all directions, like a dome over a platter. For long stretches, the scene repeats itself – eerily perfect rows etched in the dust of empty fields, depleted for the season, without trees or signs of human habitation. Land that was once the province of cotton plantations and family farms is now held in huge parcels by mega-corporations, and

Day 72 Leland, Mississippi

November 3

"Daddy always tol' me, they's lotsa ways you kin have the blues. If you broke, that's the blues. If you hungry, that's the blues. If you got a good woman and she quit ya, that ain't nothin' but the blues."

every possible square inch of ground is in production. Even those who work these fields must have a long commute from wherever they live into this vastness.

A cluster of structures, the same gray-brown as the earth, emerges from the haze. If the place has a name, I miss it. Grassless yards, littered with trash and junk, surround tumbling-down houses. A split and rotted pickup seat oozes stuffing in a front yard and a dog sleeps beside it in the dirt. I don't want to imagine anyone lives there.

I see the child, then, standing in the doorway, watching me pass. A screen door dangles from one hinge, framing the child in a wedge of weathered wood and peeling paint. Boards are haphazardly nailed across screenless windows and the front step is an upturned cooler.

She or he is barefoot on this cool November morning, wearing only a too-big pair of shorts that hang on a pencil-thin, gray-brown body. Black eyes stare back at me, and what I feel in those few seconds breaks my heart. There is no hope or desire or curiosity, no bravado – not even desperation. There is no child left in that child. Those eyes are dead, defeated and resigned from a cruel and non-responsive world. Life stops in a freeze-frame. All I know to do is to choke out a prayer for a miracle to find that child.

After a few more random turns, I unwittingly end up rejoining Highway 61, which in these parts is known as "the Blues Highway." It carries me into Leland, Mississippi, where a boulevard of once-grand old homes

bears witness to better times. The rest has the scruffy, beaten-down look of another Delta town that has been losing jobs to agricultural mechanization for decades.

Until I pass it, I had forgotten about the Highway 61 Blues Museum here. When it registers, I make a U-turn in the deserted street. A man in a straw hat leans near the entrance, having a smoke. He greets me with a big smile and some words I don't quite catch, then snuffs out his cigarette and follows me inside.

He is Pat Thomas, he tells me, and his father was the well-known bluesman and folk artist, James "Son" Thomas. He likes to come here a few times a week, he says, just to see who might stop by.

I look around the small museum and then, since I am the only visitor, we settle onto stools in front of the display about his father and he begins to talk. I miss some of his words at first because my ear is unaccustomed to his deep Mississippi accent and vernacular, but I understand his infectious grin and something I can't quite name in his piercing hazel eyes.

He didn't need to know how to read, he says, "cuz you cain't learn it from no book nohow." His father taught him to sculpt and to find the clay along the river banks and to draw, using any materials they could find. He learned to play the Blues, he says, just by watching his father's fingers.

"Daddy always tol' me," he says, "they's lotsa ways you kin have the blues. If you broke, that's the blues. If you hungry, that's the blues. If you got a good woman and she quit ya, that ain't nothin' but the blues. Sometimes, I get a happy blues feelin'," he continues, "and sometimes I get a mad blues feelin'. It just somethin' that come in ya – ya gotta feel it."

He gets very quiet when he talks about his father dying in 1993 and says that for a while, he couldn't play and, "I just hadda leave that guitar alone. But then," he says, "I started feelin' kinda shamefaced and I knowed I hadda put my heart there for my father." Now, Pat mostly plays the old songs, just like his father did. "Sometimes," he says, "I go to the graveyard and play and it seem like he kinda wakes up. But then," he continues, "he just git back down in that hole o' his."

He takes up his guitar then and plays and sings for me, and I know I am hearing the *real* Delta Blues as it was heard on porches on sultry summer evenings. The simple, repeated lyrics tell of love gone bad, but beneath that is a soul's *need* to sing, to sustain a body through a life of hard work and oppression. We can listen to the stories, see photos and visit museums, but only those who lived it know what it was like to be black in a segregated South. This is the music of such souls.

It's tough to describe Pat Thomas. He is some mixture of wisdom and innocence and keen perception. When he smiles, his whole being is transformed and when he laughs, his whole body participates – and, there is something more going on, something mysterious behind those hazel eyes.

When it is time to go, Pat draws a "diamond-eyed cat" for me and says to keep it with me for good luck. "It's got hoodoo magic," he says, with no trace of a smile. I can't say I understand much about hoodoo, only that it is different than voodoo and that it originated here in the Delta among slaves. When he hands me the drawing, though, and looks in my eyes, I get goosebumps.

So, I tape my diamond-eyed cat to the dashboard and let it ride shotgun a while.

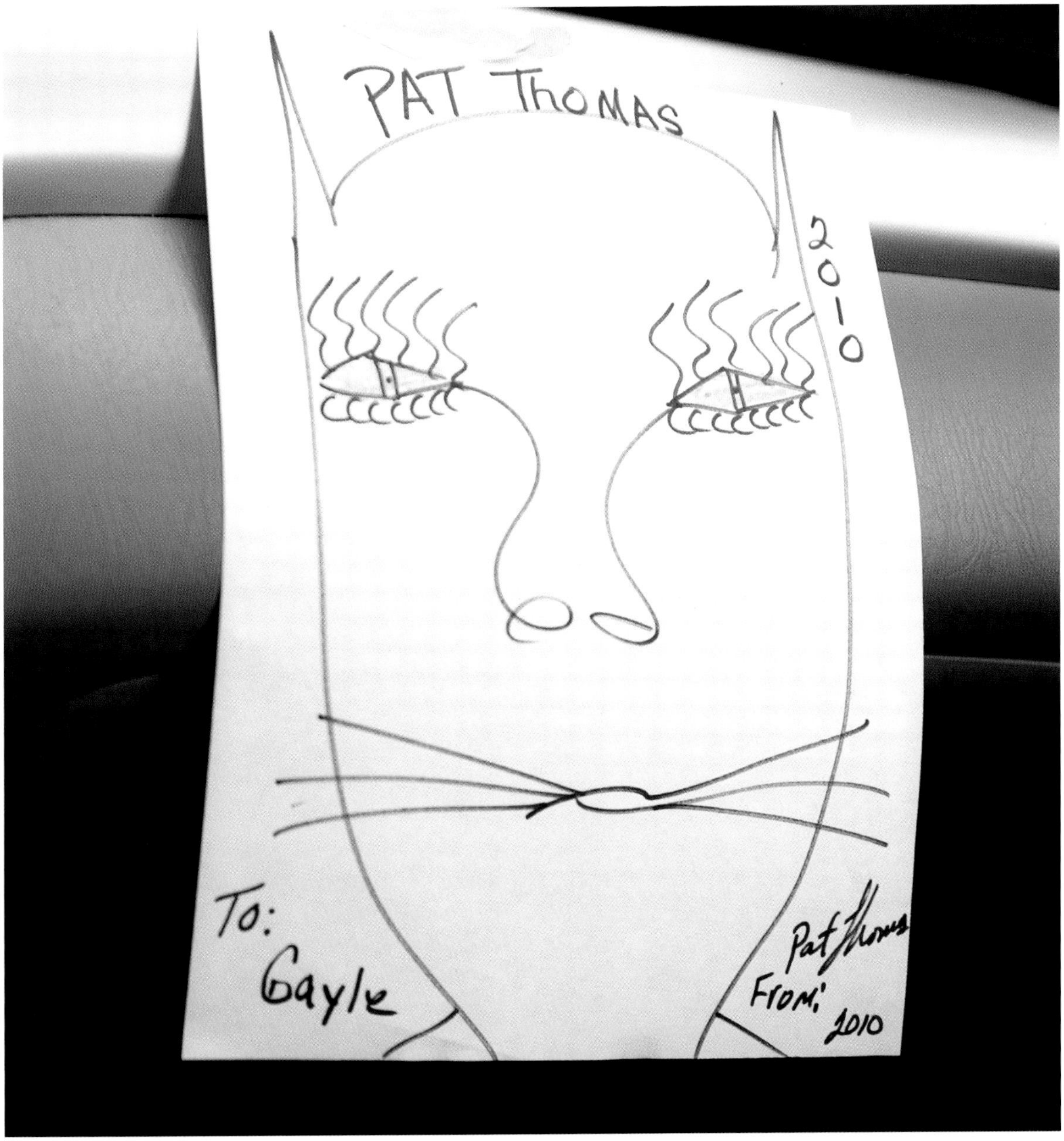

On the Way to Work...

The Lower Mississippi is much less accessible than the Upper River. Towns, for the most part, are securely barricaded behind levees and floodwalls, and River parks and vantage points are more scarce. The Great River Road is often miles away from the River itself and smaller roads often dead-end into swampy lowlands. The Lower River is so wide that bridges are a major investment, so they usually occur only at sizable cities that might be separated by a hundred miles of River. When you do reach a bridge, it is often four or more lanes of fast-moving traffic, allowing only fleeting glimpses of the River as you cross.

So, I am thrilled when I see my home for the next two nights in Vidalia, Louisiana. The Comfort Suites Hotel is fearlessly cozied up to the River and my room has a huge picture window for watching it. You might imagine that, at this point, I would be complacent about a view of the River, but I'm as tickled as a 7-year-old as I settle in for the evening.

You might even think that watching a barge ply the River would be old hat, but not so – I can't resist them! They have a way of sneaking up on you, and the deep vibration of the engine is subtly felt before it is heard. It's a busy River here and I feel/hear them even with the heater fan running, so I am out of bed a half-dozen times before I fall sound asleep.

I have promised myself a day to catch up on business and, although I had given myself permission to sleep in, I am bright-eyed and packing my gear at 5:00 a.m. Sometime in the night, it dawned on me that day 75 means only 15 remaining sunrises on this journey – I can sleep when I get home! So, I am out on the Riverwalk while the sky is still black, marveling for the gazillionth time at how placid and serene the surface of the River can be while moving something close to 4 million gallons of water per second.

The River begins to shine a soft pewter, reflecting light I can barely see. I take the path to the base of the

“The Great River Road is often miles away from the River itself and smaller roads often dead-end into swampy lowlands.”

twin cantilever bridges linking Vidalia with Natchez, Mississippi.

They are called "twins," and from here they look like it, but they are not. The span that carries westbound traffic was completed in 1940, and was a major accomplishment of the Works Progress Administration (WPA). It was built to endure and is the tallest bridge in Mississippi, allowing a clearance of 125 feet for boats and barges. It is, however, shoulder-less with only two 8-foot lanes, so it requires that one pay attention, given the size and speed of today's vehicles. With complements to the decision-makers of the time, when a new bridge was needed, it was built to match the old one, except it has 11-foot lanes and shoulders, so it comfortably carries the higher volume of eastbound traffic.

As soon as it is light enough to do so without breaking an ankle, I store the camera in the backpack and clamber across the rocks and chunks of broken concrete to the water's edge, and dip my fingers in the cold water. I take out the leather pouch of sage that has been with me since my Minnesota friend, Terry, gave it to me and, as he asked me to do, sprinkle some on the water as a gesture of appreciation. The commanding force of nature before me looks nothing like the tiny River of northern Minnesota, but it has changed only in appearance – it feels the same to me.

There is a swath of soft peach at the horizon now and then light blue into dark blue into indigo over my head and the River mirrors it all. I am happy. Not happy *because*…just happy.

Out on the levee, a family of foxes bounds toward the woods, followed by a doe and her fawn, all accompanied by a symphony of birds. A rough and muddy, but I think doable, road descends from the levee to a small lake that appears to be dotted with white birds. God bless my faithful Highlander, we slurp and churn our way down.

I leave the car and tromp closer, as stealthily as mud-caked boots will permit. The birds allow me surprisingly close and, through my big lens, I watch scores of Great White Egrets and a couple of Great Blue Herons fishing, preening and high-stepping it around the shallow lake. The branches of gold and amber-tinged trees rimming the lake are lined with the black shapes of dozens of Cormorants. I move a little closer and stand quietly – I know they are aware of me, but they do not seem to mind.

Back in town, I pass the Vidalia Police and Fire Station and, although it's slow to register, I glance back to see a photo op that stops me. An officer is raising the flag, in a scene bathed with golden light and completed by a vintage truck. By the time I turn around and go back, the flag is flying high and the officer gone. I hesitate just a moment, then walk inside.

Eight or ten officers surround a coffee and doughnut laden table in what must be their morning meeting. They are startled to see me and have that "ready for anything" look, so I quickly apologize for the interruption, explain what I am doing and what I saw, but was too slow to catch. Hearty laughter fills the room and the flag-raiser is prodded with, "Get on out there and do it again, man!" and, "Go! It's your chance to be a star!" He cheerfully obliges.

And *that* is my morning commute to work. Armed with fresh coffee, I assemble my breakfast and portable office on the table by the window. Happy day 75!

Best Friends Forever

Natchez, Mississippi, sits on its high bluff as prettily as a Southern belle on her parlor chair. Before I do anything else, I drive the streets lined with sumptuous antebellum mansions and gawk. Some of these grand homes are open for tours and some are inns or B&Bs, but many are still private residences, often occupied by descendants of the original owners. Somehow, the Old South seems to have survived in Natchez, and not just as a show for tourists.

In the prosperous years prior to the Civil War (which around here is sometimes called "The War of Northern Aggression"), plantation owners, whose cotton fields sprawled across the surrounding lowlands, brought their families to live in Natchez. Here they found safety from flooding, a steamboat landing and the society of other planters.

Although the city was occupied by Union troops during the war, it was spared the destruction seen in much of the South. As a result, Natchez now has more than 1,000 structures on the National Register of Historic Places, creating a sort of time capsule that draws more than 700,000 visitors each year.

All this opulence and heritage brings a first impression with a tinge of exclusivity, but our Moms were right, of course, when they warned against such judgments. My first contact with a "Natcheezian" proves that.

A steep drive leads to a sweeping view of the River. As I am admiring it, a woman jogs up the sidewalk and greets me so warmly that, for a second, I wonder if we have met. When I return her greeting, she stops and we chat. Four minutes later we have covered enough ground that she is prepared to introduce me to another neighbor who comes along. Ten minutes more and the three of us are in the first woman's car, heading to see

"It is an antique now, and it is so precious to us that we keep it under a glass dome. It's up to whoever had the last wedding to keep it safe and that is very unnerving!"

"Magnolia Vale," an antebellum home that her brother is restoring. So much for first impressions.

Tommy Polk was already a friend before we see each other for the first time. When he heard about the 90-day journey before it began, he called me to offer his help. Now, as he shows me my home for the next two days, being in his company feels as comfy as an old shoe.

The little row house, built in the 1880s for millworkers, is now a delightfully funky guesthouse called "Shanty Bellum." With its pink exterior, the mantle dripping with Mardi Gras beads and the turquoise walls covered with guitars, music posters and Tommy's songwriting awards, it feels like a Key West beach cottage. There are even Moon Pies atop the bed pillows!

When Tommy introduces me to his girlfriend, Elodie Pritchartt, the two immediately invite me to join them at a cookout at the bluff-top home of a friend. So it happens that I find myself on a glorious fall evening with a party of colorful, eclectic friends, talking and laughing. As the setting sun turns the River into a luminous swath of silver and rose, I can't help standing back a bit and marveling at how people from North to South have continually opened their hearts and invited me into their lives. If you should ever find yourself feeling jaded or discouraged or cynical about the basic goodness of people, an experience like this would be the cure. I am amazed every day by the kindnesses offered.

Mrs. Mary Ann Brandon Jones is known to most people in this oh-so-Southern town simply as "Miss Jones." Something about the way Tommy speaks of her makes me ask to meet her. A call is made and, without hesitation, she invites me to visit. Still beautiful at 84, Miss Jones is also funny, spunky, warm and elegant in a completely unselfconscious way. Over iced tea, in a sunny room overlooking her garden, she

Reprinted with the permission of Mrs. Mary Ann Brandon Jones.

tells me stories of her life and of her family's long history in Natchez.

Among them is this. "These are the Garter Girls," she says, as she hands me a black-and-white photo of seven leggy, swimsuited girls, posing glamorously with pointed toes and dangling cigarettes. "It was taken during World War II," she says chuckling, "for one of our boys overseas. We were all good friends," she continues, "and daughters of the ladies who founded the Natchez Garden Club – that's me on the far left."

It was later that they became known as "The Garter Girls," when the first of the seven friends married. A family friend gave her a garter for the occasion and stipulated that it must be passed on to the others when their turn came. All the girls married locally, raised their families in Natchez and remained friends through the years. When their daughters began to marry, the garter was passed to them and now it is being worn by their granddaughters.

"It is an antique now," she says, "and it is so precious to us that we keep it under a glass dome. It's up to whoever had the last wedding to keep it safe and that is *very* unnerving! In fact," she continues, "when it was my turn, I was so nervous that something might happen to it that I actually kept it in my safe deposit box!"

"There are just four of us left now," she says, "and one has Alzheimer's. We visited her on her birthday and took balloons and cake. You couldn't tell how much she understood, but we could tell she had fun."

I have a group of girlfriends like this – and listening to this beautiful story, I feel them with me. We call ourselves "The Gills." Best friends for 30-plus years, we gather for birthdays and for our slightly infamous annual pontoon float trip. The amount of food and drink we haul aboard challenges the boat's capacity and for nine solid hours we laugh, swim, talk, eat and repeat. We have been through *everything* together – we know each other's glories and foibles and, most importantly, we know that we've got each other's backs. This one's for you, my friends – and for girlfriends everywhere!

I climb the hill again for the 77th sunset. Sometimes, I am asked if traveling alone gets lonely. Not possible, I say – I seem to always be in the company of friends.

Chapter Eight: Sugar Cane and Ships

“In the way that a stooped and wrinkled old woman is the same person she was when her body was svelte and her skin satiny, the Mississippi River is always the Mississippi – and, the changes are undeniable.”

– Gayle Harper

Kindred Spirits

Tara is the first to greet me when I arrive at Cottage Plantation in West Feliciana Parish, Louisiana. When I open my car door, her big white head is in my lap. "Well, hi there," I say, surprised, which is enough to make her dance with joy and wag the whole back end of her body, as if her favorite person has finally arrived. She shadows me on every trip to the car and then waits outside my door, as I settle into my antique-filled room.

As dusk creeps in under the trees, Tara happily accompanies me as I explore the surprisingly intact plantation grounds, including an old school house, the milk house, the carriage house, slave quarters and the old walled cemetery.

As twilight gives way to darkness, Tara's head is in my lap as we sit on the broad gallery surrounding the antebellum home. I am stroking her velvety ears and she occasionally moans in ecstasy, as if this has been our evening ritual for decades. I have no idea where she usually sleeps, but when I open my door to see the moon on a 2:00 a.m. trip to the bathroom, she is there, instantly alert and ready if I am.

Just before sunrise, I look out again to see a world shrouded in dense fog, my favorite weather for photography. I am out the door in minutes, much to the delight of my friend.

Like an illustration in a scary fairy tale, massive, gnarly branches of ancient live oak trees reach out into the dimness, twisting and arching and then drooping heavily to the ground. Long, gray-green beards of Spanish moss hang motionless, the atmosphere too thick for even the slightest stirring. The air is a rich concoction of scents that I cannot distinguish – slightly spicy and sweet and extravagantly fertile. A strange, soft call of some unfamiliar insect or frog echoes in the woods, mingling with muffled birdsong.

“The air is a rich concoction of scents that I cannot distinguish – slightly spicy and sweet and extravagantly fertile.”

Beneath and within it all is a silence that is alive and listening, pregnant with potential and with memories. Everything is simultaneously simplified and amplified. Tara leads the way down the mile-long lane, vanishing like a ghost-dog if she goes too far and then reappearing, waiting, watching me intently, tail slowly waving.

Muted beams of light now penetrate the canopy, pooling on the ground and bringing contrast to our monochromatic world. We are both a little tired, I think, and the mystery is waning as morning comes on. I think of coffee and head home. Tara flops down with a thump in front of my door, as I step onto the gallery. There, on the wicker table, is a still-steaming cup of very black coffee in delicate china on a silver tray – a resplendent gift from some unseen angel!

Sparky, the black cat, ambles by and gives Tara a nose-nuzzle and me a shin-rub, before continuing on about his business. I have neither seen nor heard any other humans since Miss Frieda checked me in, although she said there is one other guest, whom I will meet at breakfast.

This alluring B&B is, I am sure, buzzing with guests in other seasons, but on this mid-week morning in mid-November, it seems to belong to Tara and me.

Nottoway

In the way that a stooped and wrinkled old woman is the same person she was when her body was svelte and her skin satiny, the Mississippi River is always the Mississippi – *and,* the changes are undeniable.

It is dirty. Its familiar, earthy scent now has sharp, caustic undertones. Its traffic is intimidating. Although occasional small boats do brave this stretch of River between Baton Rouge and New Orleans, it is primarily the province of towboats pushing flotillas of forty or more barges and of ocean-going tankers and cargo ships. These industrial gray, no-nonsense giants with often unpronounceable names look absurdly oversized on the River and give no hint of the cargo that stuffs their bellies as they push toward the port of Baton Rouge.

Refineries and chemical plants butt up against each other on the River banks. Trees and marshlands have been replaced by bizarre conglomerations of colossal holding tanks and strangely-shaped metal structures fed by miles of gargantuan metal pipes. The River's natural sinuous shape is no longer visible – straight cuts of channelization have eliminated her curves. Continuous levees as tall as three or four-story buildings squeeze her like a corset.

The River that has been my friend and companion all these weeks has been greatly altered and seems imprisoned, although we know she will always retain the power to break free when necessary.

Behind the levee, cotton fields have given way to verdant fields of sugar cane, with long, slender leaves arching from plants taller than I am. Sugar, which was often called "white gold" in the half-century prior to the Civil War, was a favored luxury item that brought fabulous wealth to the plantation owners of this region.

When the land was plotted here, it was usually into long, narrow parcels that allowed each to have River frontage. As a result, this section of River was once like a boulevard, passing one grand plantation home after another. Most of those great houses fell into disrepair in the crushed economy that followed the Civil War, but some survived and have been restored to glory. Today, south Louisiana's Great River Road is once again legendary for its collection of magnificent antebellum homes.

I take up my camera and wander the halls, peeking into open rooms. There are countless bedrooms, a spectacular white and gold ballroom, a dining room where the table is set with 1830s French porcelain on silver warmers, a music room, a library and even a bowling alley.

I join a tour group and the mansion's story comes alive. Completed in 1859, Nottoway was home to John and Emily Randolph and their eleven children. It is built of virgin cypress and of bricks, handmade and baked in kilns by some of the family's 500 slaves.

Randolph, an astute businessman who made a fortune in sugar, spared no expense and overlooked no detail in the construction of his castle. Brass and crystal chandeliers hang from 15-foot ceilings and each of the 11-foot doors has hand-painted Dresden porcelain doorknobs and matching keyhole covers. There are twelve hand-carved Italian marble fireplaces and over 200 windows. Since each Randolph child was given his or her own servants, there is a system of levers connected to silver bells, accessible from any room. It was a lifestyle of wealth and privilege that is beyond comprehension.

Nottoway Plantation is stunning, shocking actually, for one who is not prepared for the sight. I knew it was the largest remaining antebellum home in the South and I expected it to be splendid, but I didn't really *get* it.

I check in at a small, separate building on the grounds and a porter is called to escort me. I follow him into a garden, still flourishing in mid-November, and my first sight of the white castle of Nottoway stops me like a head-on truck. It is a 64-room, 53,000-square-foot vision of grace and elegance, surrounded by towering pillars and broad, curved balconies, unlike anything else.

He leads me into the main house and up two flights of wide, curving mahogany stairs. "This is your room," he says, throwing open a door, "the Master Suite." I bite my tongue to keep from asking, "Are you sure?" and step inside the spacious room furnished with museum-quality antiques. The canopied bed is hand-carved rosewood, topped with elegant linens and an antique bed warmer. "The bed posts," he explains, "are hollow and were likely where the lady of the house hid her jewels during the war." I had no idea to expect this and am nearly speechless as he orients me to the lavish room.

"How did the bringers of tea and the sippers of it perceive one another?"

In the garden, a small army of workers is preparing for a wedding. Delicate white fabric is being draped on a canopy and flowers are appearing everywhere. It will be exquisite with the white-pillared mansion in the background, so I glance around for someone in charge. At the center of a swirl of activity is a woman I think must be the mother of the bride, giving instructions and answering questions. I watch for an opening and then approach with my own question and she happily gives me permission to photograph the proceedings.

The warm, soft light of a spectacular autumn evening seems like a visual representation of love as it washes over everyone and everything. It is a Jewish wedding and, since I have never been to one, I am intrigued by the traditions and delighted by the Rabbi's explanation of them. I drift around the periphery, careful to stay out of the wedding photographer's shots and feeling about as happy as the bride to be shooting all this loveliness without stress or obligation.

As the approaching twilight turns the sky to sapphire and golden lights glow from inside the mansion, I race from one angle and composition to the next, marveling at how harmonious and pleasing the architecture is from every vantage.

When darkness is erasing the last tinge of color from the sky, I come upon the Randolph family cemetery. Behind an iron fence, their gravestones are softly illumined against the blackness beyond. I try to gather what I have learned into an image of what their lives were actually like. I see them sitting on an upper balcony, watching steamships puff and churn on the pristine Mississippi River and ringing for servants to bring tea.

I try to reach in my imagination and put myself inside the characters of my vision. How did the bringers of tea and the sippers of it perceive one another? What was in their hearts and minds in that moment of interaction? There are no answers in the graveyard silence. Any thoughts I assign them are my own assumptions, based on the context in which I live, which is too far removed from theirs.

A pale half-moon hangs low in the western sky. It will vanish soon, leaving the night even blacker. Something about the moon's unconditional glow quiets my mind's urge to leap into absolutes and judgments.

The moon will return and spread its soft light equally on our creation of beauty and our destruction of it, on our love, our kindness and our cruelty, because its nature is to shine and it has no capacity to judge.

Sweetness

Military-straight rows of exotic-looking sugar cane stand tall on both sides of the road. A sudden breeze crosses and the long, graceful leaves rise to it and fall again as it passes, a wave on a green sea. I pull over and walk to the edge and stand listening to the murmuring rustle. I step inside and am swallowed by a towering jungle, which, in spite of its regimented rows, feels a little wild.

On the road again, I come up behind a semi-truck pulling a mesh-sided trailer heaped with stalks of sugar cane about three feet long. I could pass, but I'm curious about this crop, so I follow, watching as if the moving hill of cane might answer my questions. Lost in my musings, I pass a field being harvested before it registers – when it does, I pull over and walk back.

To my left, the dense jungle has been utterly flattened; to my right, it bobs gaily in the breeze, oblivious to the combine methodically chomping its way toward it. A long neck extends up and out from the belly of the combine, with two heads spitting out the remains – one into a bin pulled by a tractor and the other into the air and onto the naked field beyond. The tractor

Day 83 White Castle, Louisiana *November 14*

“A sudden breeze crosses and the long, graceful leaves rise to it and fall again as it passes, a wave on a green sea.”

and combine move as one, like a team of horses long accustomed to pulling together.

When the bin is full and the tractor pulls away, I wave at the combine. I can't see into the cab to know if anyone waves back, but I assume so. It looks like it will take a while for the tractor to deliver its load and return, so I start out across the field, which turns out to be more challenging than it sounds.

Stubble from the just-mowed plants stands up on ridges and everything is covered with a thick layer of loose cuttings. I make very un-graceful, teetering, and I'm sure comical, progress. I look up to see the farmer on the catwalk of his elevated cab, waving and smiling encouragingly, so I keep going. Eventually, I find my technique and make it out to the amused farmer watching from his perch.

When I explain who I am and why I have trudged across his field, he smiles and nods as if he has been expecting me and climbs down. He is Randy Rivere and he is the third generation of his family to grow sugar cane on this land, he says with quiet pride. Then, he picks up a stalk of cane and begins to teach. “Sugar cane isn't grown from seed,” he explains as he cracks open the stalk to reveal the “eye” at its joint, “but from these eyes. A different machine will lay cut pieces down in the rows and cover them and new plants will sprout from the eyes. Then, for three years, we cut the plants at harvest and leave the root system to sprout again. After that, we let the ground rest a year before the cycle begins again.”

The tractor with its emptied bin rumbles up behind us. “Would you like to come up and ride with me?” he asks with a quick grin. (Well now, what do *you* imagine that my answer might be?) I pass up my camera case, climb the ladder and settle into the little cabin beside him. It's all pretty high tech. A GPS guides him from Point A to B and, if he should go beyond B, it will ask, “Are you alive? Are you awake?” A camera mounted below lets him keep an eye on the row, and a sensor tells him the height to set the cutting mechanism. The cane, which stands twelve or more feet tall, is cut at two levels and goes into the bin. The leaves, which are separated and blown onto the field, will later be plowed under to nourish the next crop.

As we bump along, he talks about his life with tenderness in his voice. "It's a good life," he says. "It suits me just fine." The harvest runs from late September until January and during those months, he works ten-hour days, seven days a week, in all kinds of weather. "I don't mind," he says smiling, "I like being out here and I know that, come winter, I can sleep and relax." Although Randy tells me this is an especially good year, due to great weather and a good price for sugar, it's clear that his appreciation of his life doesn't depend completely on those things.

At the end of a row, he stops to let me off and climbs down to say goodbye. Pointing to some billowing clouds in the distance, he says, "That's the sugar factory over

there. If I had someone else to drive the combine today, I would just take you over and show you how it works."

There is an easy, good-natured centeredness about Randy that tells me he takes most things in stride, including having some woman show up in his field with dozens of questions. When I try to thank him, he interrupts me, and wants to thank *me*. "It made my day," he says.

I drive toward the clouds rising from the horizon, because I promised Randy I would. Since he assured me it is just clean steam, it's easy to appreciate the voluptuous Michelangelo shapes gushing from the smokestacks. I pull over to watch them rise, morph into other shapes and eventually lose form and diffuse into the horizon-to-horizon bowl of grayness that has now moved in and eclipsed the sky.

A long double line of idling trucks waits to unload, edging forward a few feet at a time. As I consider whether to go talk with a trucker, a light rain begins to fall, convincing me to move on instead. In the next second, a sudden gust of wind rips the sky open and huge drops hammer the earth and pummel my car like a rock and roll drummer on speed.

Stalling a bit to see if the storm's intensity will lessen, I check email on my phone and yet another big, beautiful circle is completed. There is a message from Alejandra, whom I've not met in person, but is a friend. She and her husband are farmers in Argentina and she has traveled with me from the start by following the blog and posting her reactions. She writes, "You mention they are growing sugar cane where you are now. Is there any way you can tell us something about how it is grown? I'm very curious." Why, yes, Alejandra, it happens that I can!

Crawling down the highway, windshield wipers slapping frenetically, I'm squinting and leaning forward as if that will help me to see through the torrents. And, I'm grinning, at the ever-widening circles that ripple outward from a raindrop called Serendipity.

Metamorphoses

It's the kind of rain that makes you forget that sunshine ever existed. Evening was barely distinguishable from midday, but the last bit of grayness now fading into blackness is evidence that, above this sodden blanket, the sun is setting. Thunder rolls again from the distance, flattening the air as it comes, until it presses down on me and my little cottage.

Inside, the fireplace glows and a Jacuzzi is calling my name. There is a microwave for soup and a cloud-like bed that you lie *in* rather than *on*. There is a bounteous supply of dark chicory coffee and fresh fruit for the morning. Let it rain.

I ride the waves of storm through the night, floating from meditation to sleep to awareness and back again. Twice, I get up and open the door to let it in. It swooshes the room, recharging the air, and I stand in it until I am covered in gooseflesh and then plunge back under the heap of blankets and comforter. All through the night, the day and a second night, it continues. Time is suspended and irrelevant and I am content.

When it finally stops, just at sunrise, the silence is startling. The last of the clouds part and sparkling air reveals a world scrubbed squeaky clean. The spongy ground laps up the puddles, and everything that can croak or sing does so. Houmas House, the ochre-colored, white pillared mansion that was barely visible

“It's the kind of rain that makes you forget that sunshine ever existed.”

Day 84 Darrow, Louisiana *November 15*

through the rain, now glows invitingly in the sun. I will see about a tour before I take to the road again.

"Welcome," says the woman with milk chocolate skin, dressed in a slave costume. "My name is Judy and I will be your guide." She pulls off her sunglasses and gives us a smile that banishes the last of the sogginess from my bones. The 21-room antebellum plantation home has a complex history that included periods of splendor and decay until it was purchased by New Orleans businessman Kevin Kelly, in 2003. Now, after nearly a decade of extensive renovations, it is again resplendent and furnished with spectacular antiques.

As we follow Judy through the rooms, her larger-than-life personality seems to fill them all. She animates her stories by slipping into a dozen different voices and accents. She sits at the lustrous 1901 Steinway grand piano and plays and sings in a voice that makes us beg for more. She steps up to the billiard table in the gentlemen's parlor and picks off a hustler-worthy shot, without breaking stride in her narration. Twice, she leaves our small group howling in full-body laughs as she drops a quick-witted zinger, nods and walks away. She is a delight and, by the end of the tour, there is a connection between us and we linger in the kitchen.

We are still there when the next tour group comes through, so we move to a bench on the verandah. She tells me stories about growing up as the child of a minister in rural Louisiana and the culture shock of

Cry Out Loud," and shivers run up my spine. Her voice, haunting and beautiful, soars with emotion at the chorus, "Fly high and proud; and if you should fall, remember you almost had it all."

In that moment, I see with piercing clarity how these two brilliant, beautiful and courageous women are inexplicably, but absolutely, connected across the miles.

moving to inner-city Detroit, when her father took a church there. Some stories make me laugh until the tears roll and some touch my heart.

She speaks then about tough times she has seen recently and says she is starting over now, learning to be a single parent and putting herself through nursing school. I tell her about my daughter, Natalie, who is meeting similar challenges and also has started nursing school, building a new life for herself and her children. With that, Judy leans back against the bench and, after a quiet moment, says, "I have a message for Natalie and a song for her – turn that recorder back on, please."

What follows is another of the incredible moments that make this journey what it is. Judy opens her heart and pours out a message of love and encouragement to Natalie, whom she will likely never meet. Then, in a voice as powerful as it is effortless, she sings, "Don't

The Expanding Universe

I'm hanging tight to the grab bar of Michael Hopping's 4-wheeler as we bounce along a rutted path through scraggly, overhanging trees draped with vines and Spanish moss. We just met a few minutes ago, when I arrived at his home near Paulina, Louisiana, and he has something he wants to show me.

Abruptly, we emerge from the woods into a clearing and onto a broad, sandy *beach*! It's rare to come upon an open beach anywhere along the Mississippi River and, in this region of heavy industrialization, it is even more of a surprise. Yet, here it is – an expanse of clean sand gently sloping toward the River, unmarred by mud, weeds or debris, organic or otherwise.

The sand is a pristine canvas, stretched for nature's artistry – first texturized by the pockmarks of billions of tiny raindrops and then etched with graceful, flowing designs. The sand, dry now, traces the movement of the last rain as it formed first rivulets, then streams, then channels and then miniature rivers flowing home to the mother Mississippi. One etching resembles a perfectly shaped oak tree, complete with its root system, and another could be a map of the Mississippi and its tributaries. All are lovely bas-relief sculptures, perfectly lighted by the low angle of the late afternoon sun.

I ask Michael to stop and I know something essential about this man I just met by his response. He stops immediately and smiles – not an amused or tolerant smile, but a delighted one. He is pleased that I share his

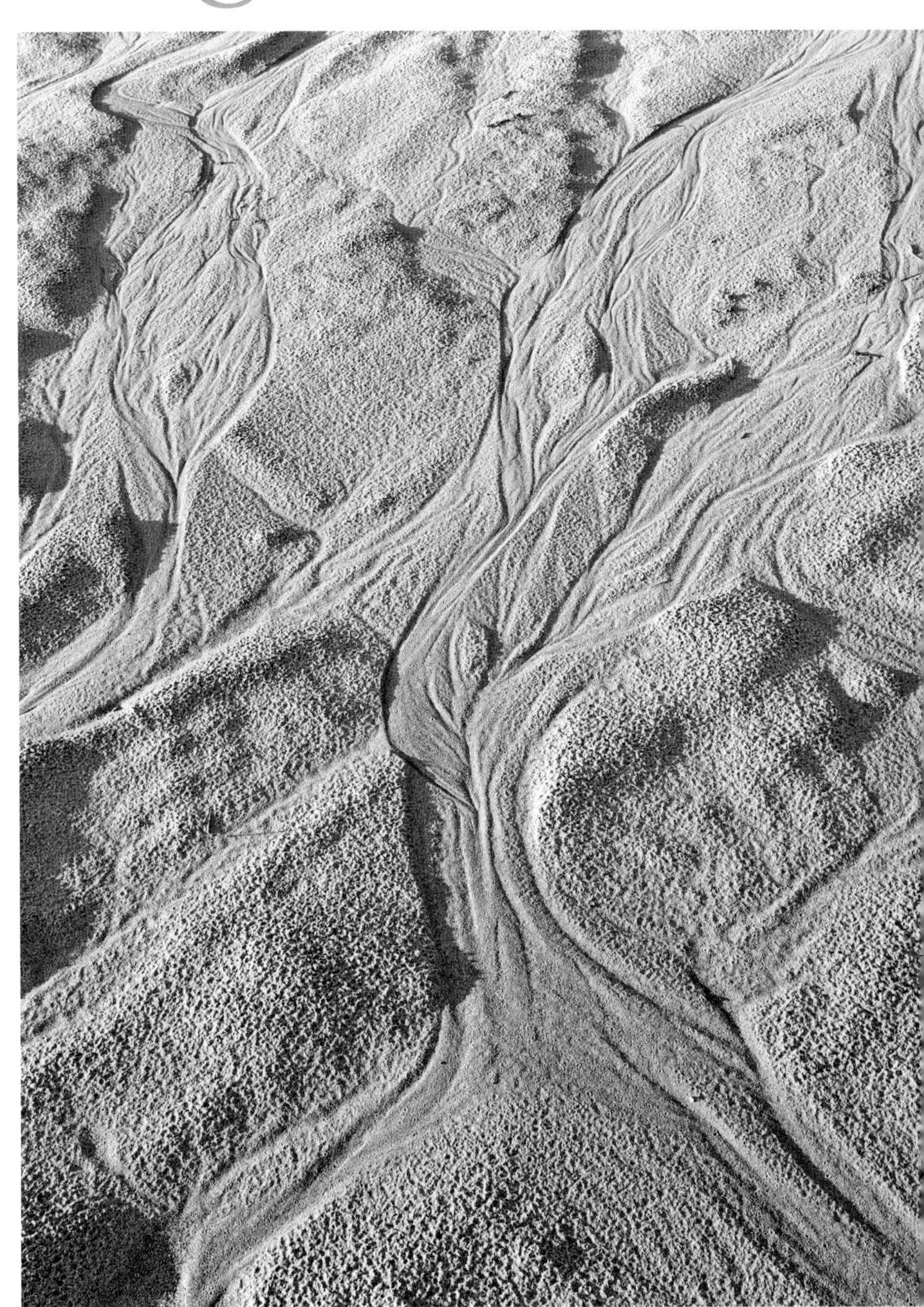

appreciation of the artistry before us. "I'll stay right here," he says, "so I don't mess anything up with footprints." He watches, smiling, as I carefully negotiate a wide circle around a design to photograph it from another angle. When I climb in again and sit beside him, I feel an easy companionship, the comfortable familiarity of friends enjoying each other's company.

We follow the levee to a small dock and Michael stops so we can watch an enormous cargo ship lumber past. Several compact, but powerful-looking, tugboats, each rimmed with a bumper of tires, are moored at the dock. I'm curious about their work and how it fits into the larger picture of the work done on this part of the River, so I ask Michael if he has time that I might go inside the small office. He looks a little surprised, but says, "Sure," and comes with me.

It is shift change and a handful of men stand around chatting, some perched on the corners of desks. They look a little surprised at first, too, but when I explain, they seem pleased and eager to tell me about their business.

The sturdy little boats are called "harbor tugs" and they are built to cut through the water quickly as they shuttle personnel and supplies to and from the big ships. When I ask, "Is there any possibility I could catch a ride on one?" I see Michael's eyes widen with surprise, but the Captain doesn't hesitate. "Yeah," he says, "I'm off tomorrow, but if you can come back the following morning, I can take you out."

"I ask Michael to stop and I know something essential about this man I just met by his response."

It turns out that, although Michael has invited me to stay two nights, he can only stay one and he will be returning to his other home in Port Allen, Louisiana. He leaves some delicious food, shows me how to close up the house and I am alone in his lovely antique-filled home. On one level, the trust and openness shown by so many people I have met is continually amazing and seems implausible in an age when fear and distrust are often described as rampant. From another perspective, however, it is only natural. It is the way we respond to one another when we are actually seeing each other as we truly are.

It is a fine, blue-sky morning as Captain Donald ("You can call me Duck – all my friends do") Mahl and I board the tug and pull out into the main channel. After all the ways I have been on this River, the thrill of it has not diminished in the slightest. The River is enormous here and it looks utterly different than anywhere else and, yet, it is always the same – always my treasured friend and always completely unknowable.

It isn't clear to me if we are on some mission, and the tug's engine is so loud that conversation is difficult, so I just relax and take it all in. Duck drives the boat from atop a little tower, kind of standing sideways and looking back over his shoulder, which somehow makes it easier when getting close to a big ship.

Once we are out in open water, he leaves the controls and scrambles up a flight of stairs to a platform even taller than his tower. There, he pantomimes taking a picture and points to me and then bounds back down the stairs. The little tug sways and bobs on the water and the platform tilts back and forth like a teeter-totter, so I am considerably more tentative in my scrambling and I keep a firm grip on the railing, but it is an awesome view.

I see a shot I'd love to get and I ask, a little hesitantly, if it would be possible to angle the boat a certain way. When the answer comes back, "I can go anywhere you like – you just tell me where," I understand that we are not on a mission and that he has done this simply as a kindness. So, I let go and play with the moment and Duck does too.

We go under the bridge and sidle up close to a gargantuan ship from Greece where I can really feel its size and wave at the sailors and puzzle over the Goliath-sized equipment that covers the deck. We pull alongside a ship from China and watch the enormous onboard crane lifting bundles three times the size of my car from a barge and into the ship's belly. We keep pace for a while with a towboat pushing its quarter-mile long flotilla of barges upriver. I am grinning with the fun of it all and the great, big aliveness of the moment, and I catch Duck grinning too.

When the ride is over, I call my friend, Michael, because I promised I would. He laughs delightedly at every detail, in the way that friends truly revel in one another's adventures.

This is it, of course – this is the answer to the "big questions" that people are beginning to ask now that the remaining days of this journey can be counted on one hand. There has seldom been time to pull back from whatever was happening and ponder what the whole thing means or how it might change me. No pulling back is necessary. Paying attention to this moment *is* what it is all about. Being fully engaged in this moment of laughing with Michael about my ride with Duck, and in every other moment in the great parade of moments, is the whole point.

Traveling anywhere means walking in the unknown. Each experience, unrestrained by the expected, expands into its full potential. Traveling alongside the Mississippi, where every experience is saturated with the River's indescribable, but undeniable, *presence*, seems to open up a whole new level of potential.

Perhaps the greatest gift of this journey may be that I now understand this is only natural – this is how full life is intended to be.

Interlude

It makes me smile to see that this is so, but I woke up this morning hungry for the road. You might imagine that by the 88th day of a road trip, a little road *weariness* might creep in, but, in fact, it is the opposite. The miles left to travel are treasured like the last in a box of fine, dark chocolates – their centers a mystery until the moment of tasting.

With my gas tank and coffee cup filled, windows cleaned and litter bag emptied, I pause, waiting. Besides my famously awful sense of direction, I made no attempt to keep track of the number of turns or their directions while searching for gas, so I have no clue where I am. The GPS is, of course, there if needed, but I love this part. I only need to relax and *feel* rather than *think* (a bit like playing with an Ouija board) and the River pulls me back.

I've seldom played music on this journey and I haven't touched the audio book that seemed such an important choice while packing. Instead, I love leaning into the white noise of the road, which, like the sound of the sea, invites me, rocks me and frees up the mind. Sometimes, my mind entertains me by playing like a child, dancing and cavorting. Sometimes, I watch it reviewing, connecting dots and seeking understanding. Then, there are the times when the whiteness opens into a deep silence and I simply rest there, watching the world like a movie. There are fifty or so miles before my next stop in New Orleans, and I am ready to savor each one.

Two sips of coffee and a handful of miles later, my attention is grabbed by a small, hand-lettered sign on a nondescript gray building that says, "Welcome Seafarers." I can't say why that is of interest and, for a few seconds, I try to resist what feels like an interruption. It is a familiar nudge in the ribs from Serendipity, however, so I turn around and go back.

I enter beneath another sign that says, "Port Ministry Center," and I am accosted by a squirrel-sized dog who seems to think she'd like to eat my leg. Her ruckus brings her humans, who offer a warmer greeting and introduce themselves as Steve Corbin, the Port Chaplain, and his wife, Ann.

The Corbins are accustomed to drop-ins and the dog has decided I am alright, so we tour the facility as

they explain their work. They are here to offer the sailors, who come from all over the world, a place to relax, play games, read, use the computers, catch a ride to the store or receive whatever practical or spiritual support they might need.

After a few minutes I think, "OK, that's interesting – it certainly shows how the ships have brought an international aspect to this quiet community," and I begin to take my leave. "Actually," says Steve, "I was just about to go aboard a ship from Myanmar that is in harbor today. Would you like to come with me?" *Aha – now I see!*

I had, of course, been curious, but I hadn't even considered trying to get aboard a ship. I knew that security would be tight and that wending my way through it, if possible at all, would certainly be time-consuming. In the company of Steve, who not only has the security clearance, but is also well-known at the harbor, it is a

matter of providing an I.D. and a signature while having a friendly chat with the officer.

Most of the ships I have seen look a little gritty, some even rusty, but as we step off the covered gangplank and onto the deck of "The Sophie," all is shiny white and blue. A smiling sailor, dressed in pristine white, welcomes us and escorts us to a large room that is clearly a common gathering area. Steve's purpose is to deliver gifts of warm hats, hand-knitted by volunteers, and, as that word spreads, the room fills with men. They are polite and gentle; they try on hats, laugh softly and express their thanks.

Neither Steve nor I speak any Burmese and most of the men have little English, but they are warm, curious and pleased, I think, to have the diversion of visitors. When it is explained to them what I do and about the journey, they laugh and nod and clap their hands together in delight. When I hand out postcards, it feels as jolly as Christmas. They gather themselves together for a group photo before it occurs to me to ask and those that have cameras in their quarters are sent scurrying to get them.

" Language is cumbersome, but communication is fluent. "

Steve explains that our visit must be brief, but that we do have a few minutes if they would like to show me around. "Yes, yes please!" is the enthusiastic response, and I am guided first to the engine room. The immaculate realm of mechanical power is quiet now and the engineer greets us formally and then stands proudly at attention. He nods and smiles repeatedly, as though he has been expecting us and all is prepared for our visit, while our guide explains what we are seeing.

Then, we ascend several flights of stairs to the bridge, the command center of the ship. After our guide respectfully asks permission, we all step into a broad, bright, semi-circular room edged with inward-slanting windows. A few people are at work stations around a room that is filled with monitor screens, controls, gauges, levers, switches and microphones.

When I am introduced to the navigator, he opens several of the drawers in front of him to show me his maps. He points to his home, Myanmar (formerly Burma), and traces with his finger the route they have traveled on this trip. Then, on a series of maps of finer and finer detail, he shows me how they have traveled up the Mississippi River since entering it from the Gulf of Mexico. I've never seen it on maps like this and it gives a much better sense of that more than 200-mile trek. He seems pleased that I am interested in his maps and he lays each one out carefully, smoothing it gently. Language is cumbersome, but communication is fluent. I understand how devoted he is to his very important job and how competently he handles it.

Next, I am invited to meet the Captain. With the same courtly elegance that I have seen in everyone, he welcomes me into his office. His English is very good and, in just moments, there is an easy rapport between us. His expressive face reflects every feeling as he speaks and his openness touches me. He talks about his job, what he loves and its challenges, including the long months away from home. "It was easier," he says, with a tone and a look that tugs at my heart, "before there was a child. Now, it is harder." I feel his integrity and I see his dedication to his crew and his job – and, now that I have met him, I see those qualities reflected in everything I have seen and heard onboard.

Steve and I have lunch in a small café and he speaks about how surprised and touched some of the sailors are to receive such kindnesses from strangers so far from home. That, he says, is his reward.

I dump my mug of cold coffee onto the grass and resume where I left off 3 ½ hours ago, marveling at this amazing world filled with beautiful souls.

Sea Pearl
Sea Pearl

Chapter Nine: The Big Easy and Beyond

"I am intensely curious about how the River will make her exit and I can hardly imagine parting company with her."

– Gayle Harper

Big/Little, Easy/Hard

Tourists like to call it "N'awlins," but on the tongue of a local, the city's name rolls and slides, smooth and spicy, each syllable savored so that it sounds more like "Neuw Awwlens." This exotic, laid-back, yet slightly dangerous city is beautiful, multi-cultural and richly talented with a mysterious and seamy underbelly – and those are just a few of the ways one might describe it. New Orleans can and will show you whatever face you want to see, while remaining authentically itself.

The first time I came here, I was a barefoot, wild young thing traveling with a girlfriend in her MG Midget convertible and our proudest accomplishment was traveling 2,500 miles without ever putting the top

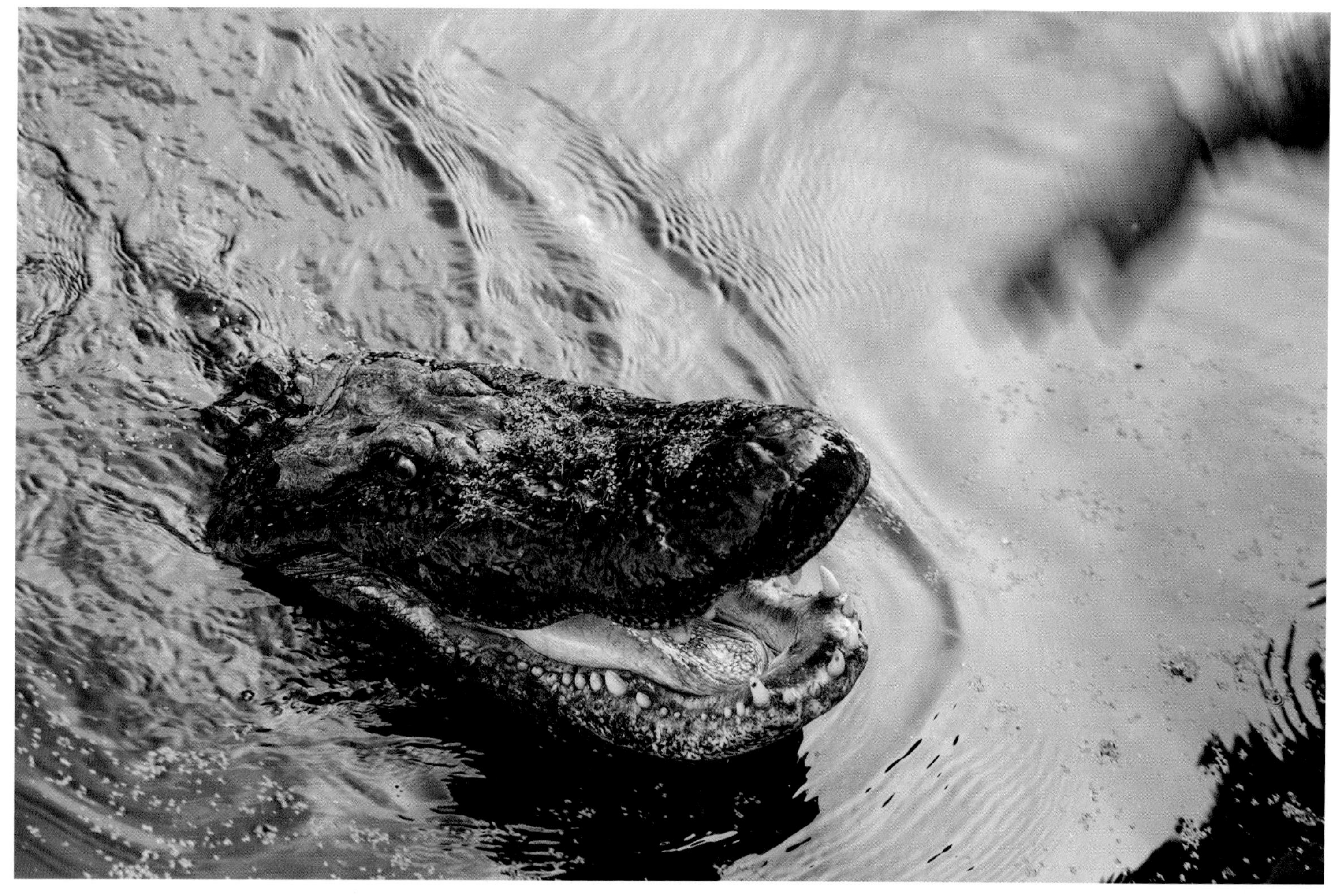

Day 89 New Orleans, Louisiana *November 20*

up. The city was perfect for us. The second time, nearly two decades later, Mike and I came as newlyweds and found it to be the most lusciously romantic city we had ever encountered.

Now, with another two decades gone, I come in the company of a raindrop. She is the ultimate equalizer, our Serendipity – nothing she passes either slows or speeds her pace. The fascination of New Orleans is equal to, but no greater than, that of Bemidji, Minnesota, or Keokuk, Iowa, or Clarksdale, Mississippi, or every foot of field, forest and vacant lot along the way.

I'm staying with my friend, Jerry Zachary and his partner, Henry, in their wonderful 1835 Creole "cottage" in the French Quarter. Mike and I met Jerry on our last visit when we stayed in the B&B he owned at the time. We had so much fun together that we stayed up talking, laughing (and OK, imbibing a bit) until the wee hours each night and we have stayed connected in the years since then. Now, Henry and I lean on kitchen counters while the three of us chat and Jerry, seemingly without effort, creates an amazing meal. It feels as if no time at all has passed – except that we skip the late-night carousing. I have an early date for a swamp tour.

The morning is *cold* – uncharacteristically so for south Louisiana, and my three jackets feel pitifully inadequate. I huddle inside them like a turtle in the midst of fifteen or so other turtle-people, all of us glum and clearly questioning the wisdom of what we are doing. The air, nearly as murky and greenish as the water, is so heavy with moisture that every surface is slippery. The boat pulls up and we shuffle onboard, as morose as a chain gang.

The group hunches together in two back-to-back rows down the center, but since I have no one to snuggle with, I go to the front. The shockingly cold bench makes me shiver as I watch my last chance to bail out recede into the fog.

Our guide, who seems an innately jovial guy, cheerfully begins a string of banter intended to tease us out of our misery, but the response is mostly glowering stares. Unfazed, he chatters on, but his Cajun accent coming through the not-so-hot sound system and the two hoods muffling my ears reduce much of it to something akin to the "Wahh, Waah, Waah" of Charley Brown's teacher.

One sentence, however, everyone seems to hear. "Well," he says, "don't know how many animals we'll see this mornin' – might be mostly holed up keepin' warm somewhere, but we'll do our best." With that, the volley of downright ugly "I-told-you-so" looks that shoots around the boat is so grim that the whole scenario suddenly strikes me as comical. I smile to myself, the guide catches it and beams back at me.

I let go of struggling to sort the distorted sounds into words and let the playful Cajun rhythm of his speech dance over me. I understand that this is his home and that he finds it beautiful and nurturing. He sits high in his seat, his partially unzipped jacket flapping against his chest, as he watches for birds, alligators or plants that might interest us. While many might see this

"New Orleans can and will show you whatever face you want to see, while remaining authentically itself."

swamp as dreary, slimy and teeming with treacherous creatures and be thankful that it isn't their home, he is clearly just as thankful that it *is* his.

The boat stops and he points toward a lumpy log. It drifts toward us and, as it emerges from the mist, menacing eyes and a powerful swish of tail make it clear that an alligator, at least ten feet long, is coming alongside.

The guide makes some sounds in a private language and the gator opens his two-foot jaws, revealing a creamy pink interior edged with dagger teeth. As the gator holds his pose, the guide leans over and, with fingers just inches from those teeth, plops in (of all things) a *marshmallow*. The great jaws snap shut and the gator turns with a sudden, splashing flop of his tail and glides away. The turtle-people who had stood up to watch, plunk back down immediately and pull in their heads, either unwilling to let their benches get cold or to let go of their grumpiness, or both.

Our guide has come prepared for them – unable to cajole away the bad humor or to spark things up with a marshmallow-munching alligator, he brings out the irresistible – a baby. The little gator is barely two feet long and, although she is lying still in his hands, those alligator eyes are on him and it seems wise that he has wrapped a rubber band around her jaws.

He offers her up to anyone who would like to hold her. Heads come up and, while some people laugh and sit on their hands, others accept the little one or reach over to stroke her. When she is placed in my hands, the sensation is surprising. Her cool, smooth belly feels soft and vulnerable and I can feel her heart beating and the expansion and contraction of her breathing. My fingers wrap around her just enough that I can touch the bony ridges of her armor-plated back. I pass her along and watch as the cloud of gloom onboard is dislodged, person by person.

Through the fog, we hear children's voices and when another tour boat comes alongside, loaded with school kids on a field trip, the man with the gator holds her high in the air. The kids squeal and scream and jump back from the railing, laughing and playing at being terrorized and there is an explosion of laughter on our boat in response.

Although I don't know the little gator's story or whether her destiny is to be soup and fried appetizers or to grow old in the swamp, I have no need to ask – her presence today has changed everyone's experience.

On cue, the fog rolls back and the air warms and brightens. By the time we disembark, people are thanking (and tipping) the guide with such enthusiasm that it seems no one recalls anything but the last twenty minutes.

The rest of my forty-eight hours in "The Big Easy" evaporates like the fog. Jerry and I have a ride on the riverboat, the Creole Queen, and he creates another fabulous dinner for a lively gathering of friends. As he helps me load my car, I notice strong emotions that, although they might seem conflicting, arise as one. I am intensely curious about how the River will make her exit and I can hardly imagine parting company with her.

After eighty-nine days of this gypsy life in the presence of this great River, I do experience the world a little differently. Moments are no longer labeled as big/small, exciting/dull or memorable or not. Each never-to-be-repeated moment, whatever the experience, stands on its own and needs nothing more. Each is precious simply because it exists.

. . . and Beyond

After hundreds of miles of snaking and looping back and forth through the South's soft soil and then sweeping low to form the famous crescent through the heart of New Orleans, the River now stretches herself out like a thoroughbred and races for the finish.

The Great River Road clings to the side of this no-nonsense River for the remaining eighty or so miles of its existence, because there is nowhere else to be on the narrow, low and wet peninsula. Although the number constantly changes, only around 35 percent of Plaquemines Parish's 2,500 square miles is dry land. The rest is some of the most beautiful and prolific wetlands on the planet.

It's a precarious place to live, called by some "the edge of the world" and those who do live here must be hearty and resilient. Five years after Hurricane Katrina left everything in ruins, many people have rebuilt their homes, but many others live in trailers and, here and there, heaps of rubble are still surrounded by yellow tape.

I pass a small cemetery and a strange sight pulls me in. Although a mausoleum and many of the headstones have been rebuilt, many others lie where they toppled, cracked or broken into pieces. Off to one side are fifteen or so concrete coffin vaults, some with letters and numbers in red spray paint, but none with names. A few have plastic flowers tucked into the metal bands securing the lids. They were washed from their resting places in the storm and are, so far, unidentifiable. A permanent sign asks that you call if you have any information.

I stand still and listen to nothing – there is no breeze, no birdcall, no sounds of any life. The two rows of displaced remains waiting silently are concrete representations of the *immensity* of the loss endured by those who live here, and the sadness that washes over me is no more than a faint shadow of their experience.

On the map, the Great River Road appears to end a few miles south of Venice, Louisiana. It feels important that I stand at that spot, so I drive straight on towards it. With no warning, the pavement simply ends. There is no signage and no view of the River. A gravel road continues around a curve and ends at the locked entrance to yet another complex of pipes and tanks. Behind a tall chain-link fence, four ravens stare down at me stoically, as if to say, "You expected something more?"

I go back and stand on the break between pavement and gravel, something in me longing for closure or ceremony. It isn't here. It feels like listening to a piece of great music without the final beat. I am suddenly tired, so I go in search of my motel.

At 5:00 a.m., the alarm jolts me from a dream that feels alluring and sensual, but my reaching for it pushes it away. In its place is a stark awareness that this is the last day of the odyssey that has been my life for 90 days. The fact that I can hardly imagine *not* living this way – constantly moving in tandem with the River, is no reflection on how much I love my life at home. Instead, it is evidence of how completely *in* this experience I have been.

Once, many years ago, as I was preparing for my first trip outside of the U.S., I was given an image in a dream. I saw myself in the middle of a river with a very strong current. It was clear to me that I wanted to go where the river was going, that it was actually life flowing. I saw three choices. One, I could try to stand where I was, struggling against the river. Two, because swimming wasn't an option against the force of the water, I could attempt to walk, stumbling on rocks and being shoved back and forth. Or, three, I could put my feet up and go with the flow.

That trip had many challenges and when things got rough, that image reappeared with the message, "Just put your damn feet up, Gayle." When I did, it became clear, sooner or later, that the challenges were caused by my resistance to going where life was naturally flowing.

In the years since then, life has shown me in a million different contexts that, however the difficulty looks, it is always the same problem with the same solution. Now, lying here in the dark waiting for the coffee to be ready, I see that, while traveling with the River these last three months, it has seemed easier and quicker than ever before to sense where the river of life is going and to put my feet up. Now that the last day

is here and I will be on my own, it's like having the training wheels removed and seeing if I can balance without them.

With coffee and camera, I climb the levee, spread a plastic bag on the cold, muddy earth and sit down under the fading stars to meet the 90th sunrise. Far beyond the River in front of me, a faint rosy glow rises from the horizon, nudging away the night as it spreads. It drips like a watercolor onto the River and shimmers in delicate threads, drifting with the current. Rose gives way to reddish and then orange and the slate gray of the River is transformed into a vibrant blue. It is a miracle, repeated daily, which will never again be exactly like this.

A low bank of clouds hanging just above the horizon catches the sun's rays and throws radiating streaks of shadows before the golden orb is visible. Then it appears, a tiny, brilliant sliver melting the horizon and then quickly revealing its round perfection that can no longer be looked at. My mind wants to tell the story that this moment marks the beginning of a new day, but in truth, somewhere on this spinning ball, the sun is always rising, while somewhere else it is setting, in one continuous movement.

Thanks to a connection made by a friend I met a few weeks back, I will spend the rest of this day on board the Sibilich family's oyster boat, *The Sea Pearl*. As Serendipity would have it, they are not fishing today. Instead, the Louisiana Historical Society has booked a cruise to the mouth of the Mississippi River, a place only accessible by boat, and I am invited along.

On the cruise, there is sunshine, a wonderful lunch and lively conversation with a boatload of interesting people. *And,* there is a sense of watching it all like a theater in the round. There is a feeling of being poised on the brink of something that I can't quite grasp.

We stop briefly at Pilottown, an outpost for the specially trained pilots who take over the controls of the ocean-going vessels as they enter the Mississippi River from the Gulf of Mexico. The skill required to negotiate the constantly changing River with its strong currents is so specialized that this association of pilots is the first in a relay of three groups between here and Baton Rouge. At one end of the boardwalk there are shattered remains of several buildings destroyed by Katrina; at the other, a new pilot's lodge stands hopefully on its piers. A permanent sign hushes visitors: "Quiet please! Pilots Sleeping!"

A few miles further downriver, the Captain announces that we are approaching the point known as the Head of Passes, considered to be the mouth, or the end, of the Mississippi River. I excuse myself from a conversation and go to a narrow walkway on the side of the boat.

When seen on a map, it looks as if there is a distinct division of the River here into three main branches, each taking separate routes into the Gulf. When seen from this perspective, at River level, there is only a vast expanse of water, interspersed with fingers of marshland. Again, I sense my longing for definition, for a distinction between one identity and another – and again, it isn't here.

"Again, I sense my longing for definition, for a distinction between one identity and another – and again, it isn't here."

Eighty-nine days ago, at the headwaters of the Mississippi River, deep in the north woods of Minnesota, I was given a gift by the first of countless River friends that have been part of this journey. As he handed me a small leather pouch he had made and filled with dried sage, he asked me to share it with the River along the way, as a blessing and an expression of gratitude. I have kept it with me and this little ritual has always been an opportunity to turn to the bottomless well of gratitude in my heart. I take it out now, lean over the railing and shake the last of it onto the River. It mingles with the dancing light of reflected sunshine and bobs away on the current.

As I watch, I think of Serendipity and I know that she is already gone. Constant change is the nature of life. The water gushing from the side of Lake Itasca in Minnesota, labeled by humans as the birth of a River, entered the lake from some underground spring that carried it from some puddle, after it had fallen from some cloud, after it had evaporated from some other lake and on and on. The raindrop now flowing into the Gulf may end up traveling the length of the Mississippi all over again. I just hitched a ride for one small segment.

Life is trying to show me something here, gathering threads and weaving them into a tapestry. When I stood on the back deck of The Phyllis and was dissolved into endless star-studded space above and below me, when I fell into the boundless wisdom and innocence in the eyes of two-year-old Hazel in Minneapolis and when I hugged my dear friend, Lil, in St. Louis and knew it was the last time we would do so, it was always the same thing being shown.

When people and circumstances come together again and again in synchronicities that sometimes leave me slack-jawed with wonder, every experience is pointing to the same thing. Nothing and no one is separate – we only imagine that is so. There is one current moving all of us, all of life. If things seem to flow easily, if all the moving parts of life seem to align in ways a million times more creatively than I could ever orchestrate, it is only because I am not resisting where life is naturally going.

Nothing in nature resists the flow of life or has any fear of change or longs to control it. Only we humans have the capacity to struggle against the current, to make life harder than it is meant to be. When we loosen our grip, even for a second, on our notion of how things *ought* to be, then lo and behold, our damn feet bob right to the surface and we find ourselves *in the flow* with life. Then we see that when life's inevitable rapids and obstacles appear, we are better able to negotiate them because we are not busy struggling against what actually already *is*. The result is simply a ride that is easier and more fun!

When we see this in the micro-sense, as it applies to our little piece of the action, that the separation of our life from everyone else's was always imaginary and false, then we begin to see how we try to separate everything in order to understand it. The wholeness of the universe is a stretch too vast for our human minds, so we try to take bite-sized pieces. We pull out a chunk and say this thing begins here and ends there, but's it's all mental mumbo jumbo. It's all an attempt to comprehend what is ultimately incomprehensible.

We will never quite get this with our minds – it is beyond the scope of our concepts and words. We sense it at times and we see how it works in life, but the whole truth of it will always be known only by that part of us that has always known and that requires neither concepts nor words, but speaks only in silence.

Tomorrow, I will touch "Home" on the GPS and let it take me there in time for Thanksgiving. Every person with whom I have shared even a glance comes with me. Every sunrise, every breeze filled with the scent of the River, everything I have seen and experienced is part of me and I, a part of it.

Sail on, Serendipity. Thanks for the miraculous ride.

Acknowledgments

This project has been shared and supported by so many people in so many ways, that it seems an impossible task to adequately thank all who deserve it.

There are all those who offered lodging, opportunities and introductions during the journey. There are those who shared themselves, their stories and their time along the way. There are those who read and participated in the blog, "Surrendering to Serendipity." Then, as this book began to take shape, others offered guidance, editing and design suggestions. At every step, family and dear friends helped by their unshakable belief that it would all come together into a book that would bring people joy.

Special thanks go to Linda Palmisano, Jennifer Ailor, Mike Jungers, Marilyn Freyer, Jeanne Heuser, Rita LeBlanc, Janene Moser, Carrie Groves, Heather Caldwell, Patrick Mureithi, Doug Sikes, Randy Baumgardner, Tim Buchanan, Juliana Goodwin, The Gills, the Tuesday Night Group, Paul Weeks, Maggie Castrey, Paula Ringer, Laura Wyss, Joanna Hurley and Bob Krist. *Roadtrip with a Raindrop* is here because of each one of you.

Special thanks, also, to every one of you who believed in this project and supported it by participating in the Kickstarter campaign. Your names appear on the following pages.

Tamara Adamson
Jennifer Ailor
Leslie Anderson
Ann and Norb Bagley
Jonathan Bailey
Cindy Baker
Silvey Barker
Carol Beal
Jaretta Beard
LeAnn Beaty
Terri Becker
Travis and Kristi Becker
Trish and Adam Becker-Hafnor
Marie Benz
Debora Biggs
Denise Bischof
Joe Blank
Tiffany Braswell
Genevieve Brennan Nauman
Jim Brooks
Laurie Brown
Robert Burke
Delores Burrington
Erin Bussard
Heather Caldwell
Maria Canfield
Debi Carnes Gatlin
Thomas D. Carver
Don Casto
Marilyn Chana
Jinna Chen
Domelnica Cibilich
Baya Clare
Paul Comeau
Nancy Cooper
Peggy Curry Gleason
Luca D'Addezio
Phil and Pat Dagnon
Judy Dasovich
Brandon Davis
Kathy Davis
David and Maryelen Dixon
Julie Donnelly
Kathleen Dower Clark
Jenny Draper
Bill Dyer
Michael Ebbers
Andrew Ehlbeck
Claudia Engman
Laura Entwisle
Tom and Jean Farrell
Suzanne Fenton
Dylan Field
Cherie Frankel
Nancy Franklin
Mary Frazier
John Freed
Connie Freyer
Lloyd Freyer
Jane Freyer
Brock Freyer
Dale and Audrey Freyer
Marilyn Freyer
Matthew Freyer
Steve and Judy Freyer
Margaret Gabriel
Nancy Gaubas
Debbie Gawrych
Ted and Cathie Gearing
Pam Gennings
Sondra Goodman and John Simpson
Clyde Gorsuch
Janice Goza
Margaret Gail Guido
Mary Hamilton
Mary Lou Harvey
Meghan Harris Freyer
Roger Haywood
Vickey Henson
Jeanne Heuser
Tony Hoeppner
Gregory Holden
Earl Holmer and Ginny Ross
Joe Hooper
Madeleine Hooper
Ann and Mike Howell
June Huff
Kali Ishaya
Tamera Jahnke
Sandra Johnson
Jim Johnson
Linda Johnson
Dorothy Joslyn

Marilyn Jungers
Mike Jungers
Irene Keller
Julie Kielts
Linda King
Clarence King
Susan Klepac
Dean Klinkenberg
Kathleen Kneedler
Lisa Kozich
Nancy Lahmers
Thomas Lane
Rita LeBlanc
Regina Leitle
Wilda Looney
Carol Loula
Kirby Maram
Stephen Marshall
Marty Marty
Susan McCann
John McCarthy
Mark McCombs
Paul and Judy McCune
Kelly Molaskey
Jane Mollison
Barbara Morgan
Todd Morriss
Amy Morriss
Janene Moser
Norma Jeanne Mullikin
Patrick Mureithi
Kay Myers
Mark Naylor
Luanne Neumann
Joann Noll
Nora Ogden
Christine Panka
Karen Parry
Leland Payton
Leslie Peck
Nancy Pfennig & Dennis Rinehart
Mary Lou Pickens
Kristy Pierce
Gisela Pollak
Jim Powell
Elodie Pritchartt
Bruce Rainwater
Charles Reifers
Agnes Reininger
Paula Ringer
Mary Rudolph
Kathy Sammon
Allen and Linda Schilter
Kim Schwane
Janet Scott
Mark Shipley
Silver Dollar City
Jeanne Simpson
Shirley Smith
Kathy Smyly Miller
Judy Spearn
Debby Spencer
Melissa St. Germain
Gary Stewart and John Shepherd
Fern Stuart
Mary Sturdevant
Dave Sturdevant
Kris Sutliff
Lisa Talley
Joy Togesen
Jon Treadway
Vicky Trippe
Valerie Turner
Judy Ulam
Patty VanWeelden
Martina Wald
Terry Walsworth
Marguerite Walters
Laura Ward
Nancy and Marvin Ward
Cathy Webb
Debbie Williams
Natalie Willis
Donna Wilson
Douglas Wilson
Neal and Jan Woessner
Tracy Wohl
Francie Wolff
Kathryn Young
Jerry Zachary

About the Author

Gayle Harper has been a travel photographer and writer for more than two decades. She knows from experience that the world is made up of fascinating destinations and remarkable people. When she turned her eyes, heart and camera toward the Mississippi River and her people, however, she was simply *captivated*.

It began with making time for little "River trips" in a crowded calendar of assignments with regional and national clients and publications and then, gradually, but inexorably, moved into making time for anything else.

Roadtrip with a Raindrop is a gift of gratitude to the River and her people – and Gayle's way of paying it forward to you.

Her home is wherever she is, but she is often at home in Springfield, Missouri, with her husband, Mike, and their cat, Louie.

Travel with Gayle on the blog, "Surrendering to Serendipity," at
www.gayleharper.wordpress.com

Join the fun and conversation at
www.facebook.com/GayleHarper.MississippiRiver

Find her on the web: www.gayleharper.com
On Twitter: @riverroadwoman
On Google+: plus.google.com/+GayleHarper

Index